easy to grow! Herbs

Good Housekeeping

easy to grow!
Herbs

COLLINS & BROWN

First published in the United Kingdom in 2010 by
Collins & Brown
10 Southcombe Street
London
W14 0RA

An imprint of Anova Books Company Ltd

The Good Housekeeping website is
www.allboutyou.com/goodhousekeeping

10 9 8 7 6 5 4 3 2 1

ISBN 978-1-84340-540-5
A catalogue record for this book is available from
the British Library.

Reproduction by Dot Gradations Ltd, UK
Printed and bound by Times Offset, Malaysia

This book can be ordered direct from the publisher at
www.anovabooks.com

The following pictures are reproduced with kind permission of GAP picture library and FhF Greenmedia, Jonathan Buckley, Paul Debois, Victoria Firmston, Neil Holmes, Gerald Majumdar, Fiona McLeod, Elke Borkowski, Visions, Julia Boulton, Mike Howes, Lynn Keddie, Friedrich Strauss, Graham Strong, Keith Burdett, Zara Napier, Maxine Adcock, Howard Rice, Juliette Wade, Vic and Julie Pigula: P.10–11; P.14; P.16; P.23(R); P.26(L,R); P.27(L,R); P.30; P.33(R); P.36; P.38; P.43(T,B); P.70(L,R); P.74(L); P.77(R); P.89; P.102; P.107; P.109(R); P.110(L); P.112; P.113(L); cover image.

Line illustration on page 17 drawn by Trina Dalziel.

Colour photography by Lucinda Symons on the following pages: P.18(L,R); P.19(L,R); P.20(L,R); P.21(L,R); P.25(T,B); P.28(all); P.29(all); P.31(all); P.32; P.33(L); P.35(L,R); P.40(T,B); P.41(T,B); P.42; P.44(L,R); P.45(BL,BR).

The Publisher would like to thank Ginkgo Gardens for the kind use of their centre.

Contents

Basics

Tools and materials

Before you get started on your herb garden, you are going to need a basic set of tools. Always buy the best you can afford. Saving money on tools is a false economy. Choose those made from stainless steel with solid wood handles. Never buy unseen, try them out for size and comfort first.

It will make a big difference to your workload if your tools are comfortable to use. Take good care of them, as well. Clean off mud and soil after use and wipe them over with a cloth before putting them away. Service them regularly and sharpen them as necessary and they will last you for years.

Basic set

Spade: An essential tool, needed for heavy digging, breaking up clods, moving soil. They come in many different sizes and shapes, which is why you need to try them to find the one that suits you best. Make sure that the tread on the shoulders fits your foot comfortably, as well.

Fork: Used for loosening soil and breaking it down, especially after digging, and for lifting plants. The prongs are either round or flat – though if you are only buying one, the latter may be more useful as they do the minimum of damage to tubers when lifting them from the soil.

Rake: Used for levelling soil, preparing seedbeds, removing stones and debris. Widths vary, but an 8 to 10-tooth rake is adequate for most purposes. It is very important to make sure the weight and balance are right for you, as it is difficult to work with one that is too heavy or cumbersome.

Hoe: You will need two types: the Dutch hoe, which has a flat rectangular blade that is used, as you walk backwards, to remove weeds, loosen soil or draw a drill; and the draw or swan-necked hoe, which has a blade at right angles to the handle. This is pulled towards you rather than pushed away, and is useful on heavier soils and for earthing up.

Hand trowel and fork: The trowel is a versatile tool, but is primarily used for planting. The fork is useful for weeding near plants and loosening soil. They need to be sturdy and well made. They come in different shapes and sizes, so take your time to find the one that is most comfortable for you.

Garden line: Essential for making sure your rows are straight when planting seeds. You can buy them, or make your own by tying twine to two short canes.

Cultivator: Not essential, but the three to five claw-like prongs are useful for breaking up ground and weeding between plants.

Mattock: This is a heavy chisel-bladed hoe, again not essential, but sometimes easier to use on hard ground.

Pocket knife: Invaluable for slitting open bags of compost or manure, cutting twine, taking cuttings, etc.

Sharpening stone: Useful to have to keep edges sharp and well maintained.

Secateurs/shears: For pruning, cutting, keeping things tidy.

Others

Watering can: Chose a sturdy one – plastic or metal – with a capacity of seven to nine litres (1½–2 gallons). You will need two detachable roses – one coarse and one fine – so you can match flow to plant.

Wheelbarrow: For moving large amounts of soil, manure, plants, bags, etc. Again, size and balance is personal and you may find a secondhand one does the job as well.

Bucket: For holding soil and liquid materials, or moving quantities of stuff around the plot.

Carrying sheet or bag: Keep nearby while working

Hand tools
Good quality hand tools with solid wood handles will last longer and make gardening much easier.

to save time on trips to the compost heap or shed.
Bamboo canes: A selection of various sizes for marking out areas or positions, and providing support for plants, nets and wire.
Twine: For tying up branches, stems, canes, wires, etc.
Gloves: Choose a lighter, supple pair for pruning and planting, and a heavy duty pair for messier jobs such as handling prickly and stinging plants.
Horticultural fleece: To protect plants from the cold or pests, or to warm up the ground.
Cloches: A variety of different shapes, sizes and materials, including glass, plastic and polyurethane. For covering rows or individual plants – useful if you want to bring forward or extend the growing season, or for warming up the soil prior to sowing or planting.
Cold frames: Used for bringing on young plants or protecting a growing crop. They can be static with a solid floor, or movable (without a floor) to offer protection for plants growing in the ground, or adapted to make a hot bed.

For sowing seeds

Seed trays and small pots: Made of plastic (though wooden and terracotta types also available) and used for sowing seeds that need to be pricked out when they have germinated.
Modules: For sowing individual seeds to grow on to the planting out stage.
Biodegradable pots: Used for sowing crops that do not like their roots disturbed. Once the seedling is large enough to be planted out in the ground, the whole thing can go in and the container will rot down as the plant grows.
Dibber: A pointed metal or wood tool used to make holes for planting seeds or young plants. A small one is used for pricking out seedlings.
Labels and marker: Essential so you know what is where. Many different types available in plastic, wood or slate with appropriate pencil or pen.
Propagator lids: Usually made of clear plastic and put over seed trays to speed up germination. You could also use cut-off plastic bottles set over individual pots.
Electric propagator: A small unit in which seeds are placed when a specific temperature is needed to germinate them (usually 13–16°C/55–61°F). The heat source may be a light bulb, heated plates or coils. Not essential, but a useful piece of equipment to have and they are usually inexpensive to run.

What to grow

Herbs – that is, plants that are valued for flavour, scent or some other qualities, which are used in cooking, as medicines, and for spiritual purposes – are fairly easy to please. Most of them grow vigorously in the wild and some may even be classed as wildflowers or weeds. The majority need little more than a sunny situation and a free-draining soil. However, as with all plants, it pays to find out which conditions your herbs prefer.

Choosing herbs

The herbs you choose to grow are very much a matter of personal taste, quite literally in the case of culinary herbs. In addition to those for the kitchen, and those for herbal remedies, a number attract benevolent insects, such as bees and butterflies, and you could just as easily make a herb garden for encouraging wildlife.

Herbs, like other garden plants, divide into those that have woody stems (shrubs and subshrubs like lavender and rosemary), soft-stemmed perennials that come up year after year, such as lemon balm (*Melissa officinalis*) and horseradish (*Armoracia rusticana*), and annuals that are grown every year from seed such as basil (*Ocimum basilicum*).

In a larger garden, herbs can be grown in their own specific border or mixed with other plants in the perennial border. How you grow them, and even buy them, will depend on which group they belong to. Generally speaking, shrubby herbs can be grown from cuttings while annuals are grown from seed.

Aromatic herbs

One of the most appealing aspects of many herbs is that they smell so good in the garden, especially when they are brushed against as you walk past them.

Siting aromatic herbs
Plant aromatic herbs in a prime position, such as either side of a path – brushing against the leaves releases their scent.

A broad selection of aromatic herbs is listed in the section of the plant directory devoted to this type of herb, on pages 50–63.

Culinary herbs

Herbs for culinary purposes are used fresh or dried. Although dried herbs can be more pungent, when fresh they give dishes a delicious flavour, notably fresh basil with pasta, rosemary with grilled meat, and tarragon with chicken. By adding herbs to food, not only do you enhance flavour, but you also benefit from the important vitamins and minerals that these plants contain. As the types of food we eat have changed, influenced by factors such as health and convenience, and the popularity of exotic foods has grown, demand for more unusual herbs has increased. Many varieties, such as thyme, will keep very well in a dried form. However, to get the maximum benefit and the fullest flavour from herbs, they should be used fresh immediately after harvest. Plant culinary herbs close to the kitchen door to allow you to gather them while you cook. There is a broad selection of the most popular culinary herbs on pages 64–91 of the plant directory.

Medicinal herbs

For medicinal purposes, herbs can be infused or macerated. Herbal teas are made by infusing leaves in boiling water and letting it stand for a few minutes. Macerated herbs are left in oil for 10 days or so, until it becomes infused with the properties of the herb. Plants have been used for thousands of years to help ease the symptoms of illness, long before chemical drugs became available. Indeed, many of the drugs which are now regarded as common – such as aspirin – had their origin in plants. Even a small garden will hold sufficient plants to make up a basic medical kit and by drying and storing them, you will have medications to hand year-round. The herbs listed in the medicinal section of the plant directory (pages 92–121) are among the most popularly used for common complaints. **Warning:** consult a herbal medicine expert before trying any treatments, since some herbs are toxic and/or have unwanted side effects, particularly in certain illnesses or conditions.

Ornamental herbs

Some herbs are grown primarily for their looks – and there are a large number that offer striking form and colour in the garden at all times of year. In this book these herbs have been classified as 'ornamental'. A selection of the best of these herbs is to be found on pages 122–126 of the plant directory.

Herbs for more difficult habitats

There are many well known herbs that enjoy a site in full sunlight – such as lavender, thyme, rosemary and sage – but those that are suitable for more 'difficult' habitats in the garden, such as deep shade, partial shade and wetland areas are not generally recognized to the same degree. The table opposite lists a number of species and varieties that will grow well in these less hospitable areas of the garden. Full details of suitable soil, site and temperature are also given in the entries for individual plants throughout the plant directory on pages 50–126.

Organic gardening

You can help to achieve harmony in your garden by working with nature to replenish its resources as you make use of them. You can do this by feeding the soil with plant waste such as decaying grass cuttings or autumn leaves that provide beneficial micro-organisms. This is what organic gardening is all about – growing herbs, fruit, vegetables, flowers or ornamental plants using plant matter, compost and beneficial insects rather than synthetic products such as pesticides and fertilizers.

Most herbs prefer a sunny, open site, but here we list a selection of those that will tolerate other locations.

SUITABLE HERBS FOR A FULLY SHADED HABITAT

Aquilegia vulgaris
Columbine

Digitalis purpurea
Purple foxglove

Fragaria vesca
Wild strawberry

Galanthus nivalis
Snowdrop

Galium odoratum
Sweet woodruff

Gaultheria procumbens
Wintergreen

Geranium maculatum
Spotted cranesbill

Geranium robertianum
Herb Robert

Hyancinthoides non-scripta
Bluebell

Lysimachia nummularia
Creeping Jenny

Primula vulgaris
Primrose

Pulmonaria officinalis
Lungwort

Sambucus nigra
Elder

Scutellaria lateriflora
Skullcap

Trillium erectum
Birthroot

Vinca major
Greater periwinkle

Viola odorata
Sweet violet

Sambucus nigra
Elder

SUITABLE HERBS FOR A PARTIALLY SHADED HABITAT

Achillea millefolium
Yarrow

Ajuga reptans
Bugle

Arctostaphylos uva-ursi
Barberry

Chelidonium major
Greater celandine

Cimicifuga racemosa
Black cohosh

Clematis vitalba
Travellers' joy

Cytisus scoparius
Broom

Daphne mezereum
February daphne

Galanthus nivalis
Snowdrop

Gillenia trifoliata
Indian physic

Helleborus niger
Christmas rose

Hesperis matronalis
Sweet rocket

Humulus lupulus
Hop

Lilium martagon
Martagon lily

Lonicera periclymenum
Honeysuckle

Myrrhis odorata
Sweet cicely

Polemonium reptans
Greek valerian

Ranunculus ficaria
Lesser celandine

Rosa canina
Dog rose

SUITABLE HERBS FOR POND AND WETLAND HABITATS

Althaea officinalis
Marsh mallow

Angelica archangelica
Angelica

Caltha palustris
Marsh marigold

Cardamine pratensis
Lady's smock

Eupatorium purpureum
Joe-pye weed

Filipendula ulmaria
Meadowsweet

Geum rivale
Water avens

Iris pseudacorus
Yellow flag

Iris verisolor
Blue flag

Lobelia cardinalis
Cardinal flower

Lobelia syphilitica
Great lobelia

Lysimachia vulgaris
Yellow loosestrife

Lythrum salicaria
Purple loosestrife

Mentha aquatica
Water mint

Mondara didyma
Bee balm

Nymphaea alba
White water lily

Succisa pratensis
Devil's-bit scabious

Valeriana officinalis
Valerian

Buying herbs

To grow herbs successfully, it is important to start with a good, healthy plant and to plant it correctly. Always buy your plants from a good garden centre or, better still, from a specialist nursery where you can obtain expert information and advice. Never be tempted to buy cheap herbs in poor condition.

Check the plants over thoroughly and avoid any that are limp and drooping, with sparse stems and just a few pale or discoloured leaves. Look closely for any signs of disease or insect infestation and make sure that the soil has not dried out and shrunk away from the sides of the pot. If there is a mat of roots producing from the base, this is a sign that the plant is rootbound and should have been repotted long ago. Having chosen a healthy specimen, take it home carefully. Carry it upright at all times and protect it from the risk of pieces breaking off. Do not leave it in a hot, airless vehicle for any length of time. When you arrive home, take it outside straightaway and water it thoroughly before planting as soon as possible. Herbs are not difficult to grow; they are tolerant of most conditions and, being strongly flavoured, they are not particularly attractive to slugs, snails and other pests. Given good conditions, you can achieve impressive results in a single season.

To summarise, here are some top tips for buying fresh herb plants:

- Decide what type of herbs to purchase. If you are looking to plant a live herb garden outside, it is important to read up on what types of herb grow in your area, soil and climate.
- Check your local farm shop or fresh produce market, which often sells healthy herb plants that have not experienced the trauma of transportation.
- Check your local garden centre if you can't find a farm shop or if you want more exotic or a larger variety of herbs.
- Make sure the herbs you choose are healthy. The leaves should be strong, shiny, green, and not browning, yellowing, wilty or mushy.
- Buy proper soil or mulch for the herb plants, along with transplanting containers. It is important to know which herbs grow best next to each other to conserve as much room as possible.

Healthy roots
Tip the plant out of its pot before you buy it. Look for roots that reach out to the edges of the pot and hold the compost together; however, they should not wind round the inside of the pot or be growing out of the base of the container. The roots should look fresh and white, not brown or yellow.

BUYING PLANTS

When selecting plants, look for healthy, disease-free top growth, a good overall shape, and small roots just emerging through the base of the container. They should not be too large with lush growth, as this indicates a soft plant that will not establish well. Plants should be well labelled with both the common and the Latin name, their eventual height and spread, their flower colours, and the type of site and soil required.

Stunted growth
This marjoram has been in the pot too long, resulting in stunted, woody growth on top and old roots coming through the pot base.

Poor root system
This plant is not ready for sale. It has only recently been potted and has little root system.

A well-grown plant
This well-grown marjoram has fresh, healthy top growth and no large roots growing out of the pot base.

Large root system
The large root system appearing from the pot base indicates that this rosemary should have been planted before now; the top is beginning to die off, indicating stress.

Poor shape
Avoid plants like this rosemary, which has a poor shape, is very spindly, and will not grow into a good specimen.

A healthy plant
An excellent specimen. It has good top growth and shape, and a few small roots just coming through the base.

Designing your herb garden

Herbs are so versatile that half the fun of growing a collection is designing the garden or feature they are to make. If you want just a few culinary species within easy reach of the back door, you can grow a selection of herbs in containers or in a bed alongside easy-to-grow vegetables. The informal herb garden may look slightly shaggy and a little bit wild, but in fact grows to quite a strict plan.

If you prefer a formal style, herbs are equally adaptable. Large leaves with well-defined shapes, such as acanthus, make strong statements. Small, finely cut or feathery leaves, like those of fennel, produce softer and denser forms. Experiment with contrasting textures and colours.

Herbs have become increasingly popular for culinary purposes, and even for general medicinal use. They are extremely versatile, producing roots, stems, flowers, seeds and leaves that can have multiple uses, even when they come from the same plant. If you design the herb garden in an attractive, formal way, with the squares or segments divided into different families or species of herbs, it will make using the herbs much simpler. Herb gardens have been popular for centuries, and there is no shortage of information on how to design them, and the best herbs to grow for different purposes. Ideally, however, you should limit your ambitions to a few good, all-round culinary herbs, and some that have medicinal uses. Do not be tempted into practising with complicated home remedies: leave it to the experts, because some herbs are extremely powerful and could endanger your health.

Tiny herb garden
Even in a small container it is possible to have a variety of herbs such as marjoram, rosemary and lemon verbena.

Planning your herb garden

Careful advance planning is always worthwhile before you begin to plant your garden. Keep in mind how you plan to use the garden and how it will look in winter. Sketch a plan of your garden with any new and existing features. Use books, magazines and other gardens for additional inspiration; the planting suggestions in this chapter are also good starting points. Refer to the plant directory on pages 50–126 to help you plot heights, spreads, colours and so on. Make sure that the garden works as a whole, each area merging with the next. Select plants for each season so that your garden contains flowers and foliage year-round.

Plant in groups or singly, depending on the type of habitat and the size of the herbs being used. For example, in borders, use smaller herbs in groups of three or five and larger ones on their own; in shady areas, plant in drifts; in wet areas, groups of plants of one species are most effective.

Although careful planning is always useful, you do not need to design an elaborate pattern for a herb garden – a small, informal patch close to the kitchen will suffice if you just want to grow a few, well-chosen favourites.

For those looking for a more attractive layout, one of the simplest is based on the spokes of a wheel, with each segment being used for a different herb. It pays to put a handsome architectural plant in the hub of the wheel to give the garden structure. A clipped boxwood would be good, as would a standard fruit tree, such as a gooseberry, or a standard rose.

The design below will work as well for culinary herbs as for medicinal ones; on the whole, it is best not to mix the two categories.

Much depends on whether your herb garden is ornamental or practical. In either case, if the herb garden is larger than 2m (6ft) in diameter, ensure that the paths between the segments are large enough to walk on, so you can tend the garden easily and conveniently.

If, on the other hand, you have very little space, you can adapt the design to a large-diameter container, simply using fewer herbs in each segment.

Herbs in containers

If you have very little space, there is nothing to prevent you growing some herbs in a window box, for example. Depending on its aspect, the kitchen windowsill can be an excellent spot for cultivating a few culinary herbs, and basil (grown from seed), parsley, chives and thyme will all furnish you with as much as you will need for the kitchen from a relatively small container.

More decorative, larger containers can also be used for more substantial herb displays. Remember that some herbs are quite vigorous, so take care when you combine different herbs in the same container. Mint, for example, spreads by runners and will rapidly take over an entire container, unless you make provision in the shape of a divider. A roof slate or tile, pushed into the container, is a useful divider.

Spoked wheel design
This simple, attractive idea uses six different herbs, one in each segment of the wheel. An ornamental plant is the focal point in the hub.

Growing herbs from seed

Seed is the means by which most flowering plants reproduce themselves. Among all the methods of propagation, growing from seed is the most common. It is much less expensive than buying already established plants, although the disadvantage is the amount of time involved: it will often take a whole season, and sometimes more, to produce a substantial plant.

Herbs normally grown from seed are annuals, biennials and many of the herbaceous perennials. Herb seeds can vary enormously in size and can either be sown directly into the ground or sown in pots or seed trays and transplanted later. Seed packets will advise you on which method is most suitable for the herb of your choice. It can depend on how you will use the herb and the quantity you would like. Growing from seed is generally straightforward, but it is important to understand a little of their requirements.

SOWING DIRECT

For many annuals and biennials (details are given on seed packets), it is best to sow seed *in situ*, where the plants are to grow, since they do not like being transplanted. Most biennials should be sown in early summer to allow them time to get established before the winter; some, especially

1 Prepare a seedbed by clearing any existing weeds, making a reasonably fine bed without too many soil lumps or stones.

2 If you are growing more than one kind of herb in a bed, use sand to mark out separate areas for each type. Be careful to sow the seeds of the larger plants at the back of the bed.

Seed requirements

Seeds have certain basic requirements in order to germinate and grow.

- Moisture is supplied by moist compost or soil. Larger seeds can be soaked overnight to speed up their germination time.
- Oxygen is available in a well-aerated seed or potting compost, or in soil that is well cultivated. Waterlogged or compacted soil can cause failure.
- Warmth is required in varying degrees for successful germination. The optimum temperature is 20°C (68°F).
- Some seeds, particularly those of wild plants, require light to germinate. As a general rule most small seeds should be surface sown or only lightly covered. Bury larger seeds to their own depth.

Germination time

On average, germination takes up to 30 days, but some seeds may take 90 days or more. If your seeds do not come up in reasonable time, take a look at them to find out what has gone wrong. In some cases the seed may have rotted or gone soggy, in which case start again. If the seed is hard, it is still alive and is in dormancy, awaiting the right conditions to germinate. Seeds do this in order to give themselves the best chance of survival; without such safety mechanisms they might germinate during drought or when temperatures are too high or too low for survival. To improve their chance of survival, wild herb seeds do not always germinate all at the same time. This may give rise to erratic germination over a long period.

umbellifers (carrot family), also require a period of cold to trigger germination and they should be sown in the fall. Annuals are normally sown in the spring or, if they are hardy, in late summer. Most perennials are best sown in spring – unless they need cold treatment.

3 Sprinkle seeds over the soil. Dust-like seeds should be scattered on the surface. Larger seeds should be pressed into the soil, to the same depth as the seed size. Sow sparsely to avoid having to thin out the seedlings.

4 If the seeds need to be covered use your fingers or a small fork to work them lightly into the soil. Firm the soil down lightly and water with a fine rose to make sure the seed is in close contact with the soil. Keep watering regularly until the plants are established.

Cold treatment or stratification

Some seeds will not germinate until they have been through the low and freezing temperatures of winter. In this way, nature ensures that they germinate in spring, when weather conditions are most favourable for growth. Sow these seeds in the autumn, cover the tray with glass to protect against mice and birds, and leave it outside or in a cold frame over the winter. Germination will take place in early or late spring.

Alternatively, mix the seed with moist peat or sand in a plastic bag and leave outside over the winter (or in the refrigerator for approximately eight weeks). In the spring, sow as normal.

The seeds of some shrubs and trees, such as rose hip and elder, are contained in a fleshy coating. To germinate, the seed coat has to be broken down. In nature this happens when the seed passes through a bird's intestine. If you want to grow such seeds yourself, they should be stratified over winter, although some may take two seasons to germinate.

Scarification

Seeds with very hard coats take a long time to germinate unless you break down the seed coat so the seed can absorb moisture. This treatment is called scarification. The easiest method is to soak the seeds in warm water for 24 hours.

Where the seed coat is very hard, you may have to wear it down in one of two ways:

Scraping Place small seeds in a jar lined with sandpaper and shake the jar.

Chipping Using a sharp knife, make a nick in the outer coat of large seeds.

Do not damage the inner, soft material, the part of the seed that will germinate, or the seed may rot.

INDOOR SOWING

Because many herbs have tiny seeds and germination can take many weeks, even months in some cases, it is not always practical to sow in situ. Vermin or birds may take the seed; more usually, weed growth overtakes the sowing area, and distinguishing between weed and herb seedlings

1 Prepare the seed tray with special seed and sowing compost, level it off 0.6 cm (¼in) below the rim. Water with a fine rose until moist throughout.

2 Pour the seeds into the palm of your hand, pick some up between your thumb and forefinger, and sprinkle thinly and evenly over the surface of the seed tray. Do not sow too thickly.

Caring for seedlings

After direct sowing, always mark the area with sticks or stones or by sprinkling clean sand over the seeded area and label with the date and plant name.

If the season is windy, hot, or cold, you should cover the area with 'fleece' to protect the seeds and prevent the soil from drying out. A featherlight, translucent fibre covering fleece creates a warm microclimate and allows rain through; it also keep off birds and pests.

Seed sown indoors

Seed trays should be kept in the shade, never in direct sun. Keep them in a warm place in the house or in a greenhouse.

When the seeds start to germinate, remove the glass cover. Do not overwater the seedlings or allow the seed compost to dry out. Keep them out of direct sun; high temperatures encourage spindly growth.

Because the seedlings have been growing in a protected environment, they need to be gradually acclimatized to conditions out of doors. This process is known as 'hardening off'. For a period of two to three weeks move the seedlings from the greenhouse to a closed frame or open the frame during the day, putting them back in the protected environment at night.

Transplant the seedlings into small pots when they are large enough to handle. Allow them to become well rooted before planting.

Self-seeding

Many herbs will self-seed if the flower heads are left for the seed to mature. In any natural or ecological planting this is desirable. Unwanted seedlings can be transplanted or hoed out.

can be difficult. It is often best to germinate small seeds in controlled conditions indoors, in a seed tray rather than in the open ground.

3 Lightly cover with fine seed compost sieved through a plastic pot or sieve. Cover larger seeds to their own thickness or press them into the seed compost. Tiny seeds germinate best uncovered. Water gently with a fine rose.

4 Cover the seed tray with a sheet of glass. This keeps moisture in, eliminates the need for further watering, and prevents pests attacking the seeds and emerging seedlings. Keep in the shade.

Preparing the site

Soil is the most important ingredient of any garden, and in order to grow plants successfully you need to understand a little about its structure and composition.

Soil is divided into three layers: topsoil, subsoil and bedrock. Topsoil is the humus-rich, dark coloured layer that contains a proportion of decaying vegetation and broken-down organic matter teeming with living organisms including worms, soil bacteria and fungi. These organisms break down the organic material converting it into food that plants can use. It is from this top layer that plants obtain most of their nutrients.

Subsoil contains fewer nutrients but holds reserves of moisture and minerals and is much lighter in colour. Through cultivation, topsoil may become mixed with subsoil, so there is not always a clear division. Deep-rooting plants penetrate the subsoil for minerals and moisture and help to break up and aerate the subsoil.

Beneath the subsoil is the bedrock, which, depending on its composition, may or may not provide good drainage and can affect the pH of the soil above.

Topsoil can be considerably improved by applying organic material, which adds nutrients, lightens the soil for easier root penetration, and helps conserve moisture. Subsoil can be improved in several ways so that its structure is open, providing better drainage and easier root penetration.

Assessing your soil

In order to assess your soil, dig a hole 30cm (12in) deep in the garden and slice cleanly down one side of it with a spade. You should clearly see the extent of your topsoil, which normally varies in depth from several centimetres (inches) to 60cm (24in) or more. An ideal garden soil is a medium loam composed of sand, silt and clay with a free-draining stony subsoil beneath.

As well as finding out what type of soil you have, you also need to establish its acidity or alkalinity, as this

SOIL TYPES

The main soil types are clay, sand, peat and loam. Other soil types are silt and chalk. Silt soils have similarities to clay. They are smooth, sticky and airless when wet and need the addition of coarse grit and organic material to improve drainage and workability. Chalk soils have a high pH. They are poor and free-draining, often containing stones, and need organic matter to improve them and retain moisture.

Sandy soil Light and usually free-draining, sometimes gravelly, sandy soil is easily worked in winter and very dry in summer.

Peat soil Because peat soil has a low pH, many plants cannot grow in it without the addition of lime. It is usually fertile and well drained.

Loam soil Loam, the most common garden soil, is a combination of clay, silt and sand. It is fertile and is usually crumbly to the touch.

Clay or heavy soil Made up of minute particles, clay is usually fertile and retains moisture. It is difficult to work in winter.

may be a factor in determining which plants you can grow. Acidity and alkalinity are measured on the pH scale. The scale goes from 0 to 14: the higher numbers indicate a soil with a high lime content (alkaline), 7 is neutral, and between 0 and 6 is acid. Most soils have a pH between 4.5 and 8.5. The majority of herbs prefer neutral to slightly alkaline conditions.

If you have acidic soil, the best way of raising the pH is to add dolomite limestone, which also contains magnesium, or better still, incorporate calcified seaweed, which is long-lasting, contains magnesium and other plant nutrients, and unlike limestone does not wash away through the soil. The only way to lower the pH of alkaline soil is to add organic matter, which is slightly acid.

It is better, if possible, to select herbs that enjoy the conditions natural to your garden than to make significant adjustments to the pH value of the soil. However, many herbs are adaptable.

Improving and feeding the soil

To make healthy growth plants require nitrogen, phosphorus and potassium (NPK) and other trace elements. Plants normally absorb these substances from the soil, but in poor soils you may need to provide them in the form of a variety of fertilizers or manures (see pages 34–5).

Poor, light soils need plenty of organic matter to provide nutrients, to encourage the soil bacteria that make plant foods available, and to increase the moisture-holding capacity. Homemade compost is by far the best material, but there are plenty of other forms of organic matter, including well-rotted horse or cattle manure, spent mushroom compost, leaf mould and various waste organic products, as well as regular use of green manures.

There are various ways of improving heavy, badly drained soils. If the soil is waterlogged, special drainage will be required before any planting and it might be best to get professional help. Adding organic materials, especially compost, helps to break down heavy clay, as does planting deep-rooting green manures and working grit and small stones into the soil. For detailed information on feeding your soil, see pages 34–5. Constant cultivation of a clay soil can form a 'pan' of compacted soil a few inches below the surface, that is impenetrable to water. This can be broken by working a fork as deeply as possible into the soil or by growing deep-rooting plants that penetrate the soil, so improving aeration and drainage.

Test tubes
Put a soil sample in the test tube and follow the instructions on your kit to test the pH of your soil. The solution changes colour and can be matched to the colour key supplied.

Soil meter
A soil meter is a simple instrument with a metal probe that is placed in the soil and produces a pH reading on the dial. An advantage of the meter is that readings can easily be taken at different sites around the garden.

Planting techniques

Before you plant a new area or habitat in the garden, assess your soil and its requirements (see pages 22–3). All persistent perennial weeds must be eradicated. Annual weeds are easily dealt with by hoeing. Thorough preparation is essential. By cultivating the soil you can improve its aeration and drainage and, with the addition of organic matter, its fertility. Ideally, choose a site with well-drained and easily workable soil, but which still retains moisture in summer.

Your choice of plants will depend to some extent on the conditions prevailing in your garden, although these can always be modified, if not changed. Some plants do require specific conditions to thrive and all do best in a situation similar to their natural environment. However, they are surprisingly adaptable, especially in the garden where conditions are less extreme than in the wild.

Planting

Planting is best done in spring or autumn, although container-grown herbs may be planted year-round as long as conditions are suitable. Avoid planting when the weather is harsh or if the ground is frosted, and also during intensely hot weather or a prolonged dry period.

Prepare the soil and plant new purchases as shown on the opposite page. Herbs do not require feeding after planting if the soil has been properly prepared beforehand and garden compost, lime and other fertilizers added as required (see pages 34–5).

All plants require moisture to grow, including plants that are described as enjoying dry, hot conditions: in the wild these plants start life from seed in the rainy season and are well established before drought sets in. Water plants before planting and keep them watered in dry weather until they are established and growing.

Preparing borders and island beds

Herbaceous borders and island beds are ideal for growing a wide range of plants, including many herbs. Borders are often set against a background of some kind, either natural or humanmade; island beds are normally more central and usually surrounded by grass.

As far as possible borders should be sited in full sun, although there is no reason why your border should not be in the shade to show off woodland and woodland-edge plants. Suitable backgrounds include a wall, fence or hedge; and for a more ecological planting, a wild hedgerow, shrubs or trees. When choosing a new site, make sure that the soil drainage is good. Poor drainage restricts the range of plants that will thrive. Many herbs will not survive having wet roots, especially over the winter when they are dormant. On heavy soils, consider putting in a drainage system.

A bed that is too wide can be difficult to maintain and is complicated to plant, so always tend toward a narrower rather than a wider design. An asymmetrical border or island bed is often effective, especially for more natural plantings, providing its design is simple.

Use a garden hose or rope to outline the area. Then mark the shape directly on the grass using sand or whitewash.

If you are cutting out a bed from an existing lawn, first remove all the turf by dividing it into manageable pieces and then lifting them up with a sharp spade. If the turfs are not required elsewhere, stack them grass-side down in a neat heap and let them rot. Removing the turf removes most of the weed seeds.

Dig heavy soil or fork over if it is light, and remove all perennial weeds. Whenever soil is turned over, weed seeds are brought to the top.

Incorporate some garden compost (see pages 34–5), if available, in order to provide a balanced slow-release source of nutrients. An alternative is a general organic fertilizer; seaweed meal is suitable but may be expensive, and spent mushroom compost (preferably organic) makes an excellent conditioner but is low in nutrients. Apply fertilizers when the soil is warming up in spring.

Preparing an open, dry area

Certain garden features, such as rock gardens and gravel beds and even walls, can provide open, dry habitats for a wide range of herbs.

Paths made from bricks, stones or concrete slabs, bedded on a layer of sand, are ideal locations for some herbs, provided the foundations allow for sharp drainage. Low-growing and carpeting herbs, such as creeping thymes and chamomile, do well here. If you have little space, a stone sink or small trough is perfect for a miniature rock garden. Where drainage is poor, you can construct a raised bed with walls of brick, stone or logs, 30–60cm (12–24in) high.

After any new construction allow the soil to settle for at least a week before you begin to plant. Break up any large lumps of earth and make sure that there are no air pockets without soil around the rocks. If the soil is dry, water the area to be planted and the herbs, at least a few hours before planting. To prepare a raised bed, fork over the soil at the base of the bed to assist drainage, then cover it with 15cm (6in) of stones and rubble. Finally, fill to the top of the walls with a rock-garden soil mix of loam, sharp sand and grit.

The most suitable seasons to plant herbs in a rock garden, or dry area, are in spring or from late summer to early autumn.

Before finalizing your planting scheme, place new plants, still in their containers, in their approximate positions. Try to imagine how they will look when they are mature – how tall and wide they will grow. Remember that some plants will grow up between the rocks and others will naturally cascade over them. Also consider the effects of colour and foliage.

Where planting into walls and between rocks in rock gardens is difficult, direct seeding of herbs such

PLANTING

Fork over the top 15cm (6in) of soil, breaking down any lumps and removing all weeds. Add compost as a general soil conditioner. Thoroughly water the plant in its container well before planting, or if it is bare-rooted, soak the roots for approximately 15 minutes in a bucket.

1 Dig a hole slightly larger than the container. Loosen the soil at the bottom of the hole; if dry, pour water into the hole and allow it to soak away. Remove the plant from the pot and place it in the hole.

2 Return the soil around the plant and firm down with your hands. Water the plant to consolidate the soil around its roots. Water regularly until established.

as wild wallflower, ivy-leaved toadflax and sedums is the answer. Drop or firm soil into crevices and press or sprinkle a few seeds into it. Seed gaps in stone or brick paths in a similar way with creeping thymes and chamomile. Regularly water herbs growing in walls until they have developed strong root systems to search out moisture and nutrients.

Preparing and planting a shaded area

A shady habitat will already occur in a well-established area of the garden where shade is cast by mature trees and shrubs, or in an area on the shady side of the house or against a wall or fence.

The best way to create a shady habitat is to plant suitable trees. Choose trees that are decorative and grow to an appropriate size for the garden. Often a single tree will provide enough shade and a simple planting underneath can look charming. For woodland planting, select deep-rooting trees that do not rob the upper soil of nutrients and moisture. Avoid shallow-rooting trees such as birch, poplar, willows and false acacia, as most plants will not do well near them.

An established area is more like a natural woodland or woodland edge where shade is heavy in summer and lighter in winter. Over the years fallen leaves will have formed a nutrient-rich soil that requires no digging, topped by a leaf layer that keeps the soil

PLANTING HERBS IN CONTAINERS

Using different containers for herbs can be great fun and can enhance your garden and give it character. Check that the container can hold the soil but let water drain freely, also make sure that there are no residual poisons in tins or treated wood containers.

The Mediterranean herbs are especially happy confined in containers which get quite dry in the summer; this replicates the habitat for which they are naturally adapted – poor soil in a hot southern country. In fact, the main problem with containers is that they may not be well drained enough for herbs, make sure your container has plenty of holes for water to drain out or the roots may become soggy and rot away. In winter this is a particular problem; sitting in freezing wet soil over winter will kill a plant that could easily have survived just the cold temperatures.

An old wine box is perfect for low-growing herbs like chervil.

Old tins, carefully washed and with holes made in their bases, make characterful containers for herbs.

relatively free of weeds. These areas need little preparation except for the removal of any weeds. Woodland-type soil with layers of humus should be left uncultivated.

Preparing a partially shaded area

Light or partial shade is ideal for many herbs that enjoy a 'woodland edge' habitat including ground-cover plants and many attractive climbers. Many woodland species that tolerate full shade will also grow well in these conditions provided they are shaded from the hot midday sun.

Most gardens have an area of partial shade under or near lightly foliaged trees, shrubs or hedges or provided by walls and fences that cast shade for part of the day. Even a single tree will provide dappled shade. Additional areas of partial shade can be created by further planting of trees, hedges and suitable shrubs.

Woodland-edge plants enjoy an undisturbed soil that is covered every autumn in leaf litter. Leaf litter adds nutrients and humus, making a loose, friable soil. When creating a new area of partial shade that does not have the benefit of annual leaf fall, add plenty of organic material – particularly leaf mould – and work it into the top 15cm (6in) of soil. Add an annual mulch of leaf mould or bark chips.

It's also a good idea to match the types of plants together; so put Mediterranean herbs like rosemary and lavender together and put colder-climate herbs like mint in a separate container which can be put in a less sunny spot.

Once you have decided on which container to use, place crocs or broken polystyrene in the bottom to help with drainage and use a good potting compost to plant the herbs into. When planting up make sure there is room between the top of the compost and the rim of the container to make watering the plants easy. Although herbs will generally withstand some neglect, it is worth checking on the containers regularly, especially in the hottest days of summer when containers can dry out very quickly.

If there are enough holes for drainage, an old bath can make a suitable container for larger herbs.

A wooden wheelbarrow can contain an entire potager, providing herbs like mint parsely and marjoram as well for the table.

Propagating herbs

Growing a plant from seed is not always appropriate or even possible. A number of herbs either do not set seed or do not come true from seed. These include many varieties with variegated or decorative foliage, or particular flower colours. Also, as in the case of shrubs, producing a mature plant from seed is often a slow process. There are also methods of using an established plant to reproduce further identical ones; these can sometimes be planted into their permanent growing positions immediately. The only means of reproducing the parent plant exactly is by vegetative propagation, which is most commonly done by cuttings.

Cuttings

A cutting is a length of stem that under suitable conditions is able to produce its own roots and form a new plant. The different type of cuttings include softwood, greenwood, semiripe, hardwood and water. Softwood cuttings root quickly but easily wilt; greenwood cuttings are preferable. Woody shrubs can be propagated by hardwood cuttings taken during the autumn or early winter and rooted outside in a sandy trench.

Rooting cuttings

Most cuttings can be rooted into pure coarse sand, but for better results use one of the following mixes: equal amounts of peat substitute and sharp sand; equal amounts of peat substitute and perlite (made from volcanic rock); or equal amounts of peat substitute, perlite and coarse sand. Peat substitute retains moisture and encourages roots; perlite retains moisture and air; and sand aerates the mix and supplies bulk and density, making the inserted cutting more secure.

Cuttings must not be allowed to wilt. Take them early in the day, before the sun is hot, and keep them sprayed with a mist spray before you insert them into the cutting mix. Once they are inserted, cover the container with a plastic bag to retain moisture until the cuttings have rooted.

SEMIRIPE CUTTINGS

Trees and shrubs are usually propagated from semiripe wood. Semiripe cuttings, like this sweet bay, should be taken in mid- to late summer when the shoots are starting to ripen and become harder. Rooting hormone powder encourages the cutting to root and is available from garden centres. These cuttings will normally root by the following spring.

1 Take 10–15cm (4–6in) cuttings from the current season's growth. Strip off any leaves from the lower part of the stems.

2 Insert the base of the stem in rooting hormone powder; knock off any excess. Insert approximately 2.5cm (1in) into the compost.

3 Space the cuttings at intervals around the edge of the pot. Keep the mixture damp; cover with a clear plastic bag to retain the moisture.

SOFTWOOD CUTTINGS

This is the best type of cutting to take from most herbs. Softwood cuttings should be taken when the soft spring growth has firmed up in late spring or early summer. Take the cutting from the tip of a healthy stem; it may vary in length according to the plant. The tip of the cutting will be floppy and the base just firm enough to insert into the cutting compost. It is important to keep the cuttings moist at all times and to avoid handling them too much.

1 Select cuttings 5–10cm (2–4in) long from the tip of a healthy, non-flowering main stem. Strip the leaves off the lower half of the stem.

3 Remove the growing tip at the top of the cutting.

5 Make a hole in the cutting compost mix and insert the cutting. Firm around the cutting gently.

7 Label and water the cutting and place a plastic bag over the container to keep the cutting from drying out. Keep the compost watered as the cutting takes root.

Plant division

Many herbaceous plants and some shrubs can be propagated by dividing the parent plant. The main advantage of this method is that you reproduce the mother plant exactly (with seed there is often some variation) and are provided with a good-sized plant that will quickly establish. Select healthy specimens, free from imperfections or disease. The method of division depends on the type of plant and its root system. In most cases all or most of the plant will have to be dug, divided as required, and replanted into new soil. Fork compost into the area from which the plant was dug to revitalize the soil.

Cuttings
Every time you cut back herb plants, it is worth putting some of the cuttings into a jar of water on the windowsill. Mint plants, like these, will root easily in water.

Other methods of propagation

Sowing seed, division and taking cuttings are the most common methods of propagating plants, but some herbs lend themselves to the other techniques described below. These include layering, by runners and suckers, or by division of bulbs and corms. See the plant directory on pages 50–126 for methods suitable for individual plants.

Layering and dropping use the natural tendency of some woody plants to develop roots and new shoots at points where their stems come into contact with the soil. Suckers are produced by some shrubs and trees, such as roses and sweet bay. They originate from the underground root system or at the base of the main stem of a mature plant and may appear as leafy shoots near the base of the parent plant or as much as several feet away. They produce their own root system and can be detached from the parent plant, dug up, and planted as new plants.

Many herbs, such as crocuses or chives, grow from bulbs or corms. These multiply over the years to produce a clump that can then be split up into individual bulbs and planted to make new plants.

Clumps of fibrous roots can be lifted and divided just after flowering or in early spring to form smaller plants each with plenty of roots and shoots. Using your hands or a knife, ease or cut pieces from the outside of the dug plant. The centre of the plant can be replanted but discard old and woody centres. Once the plant has been divided, either repot the small clumps or, in the case of large clumps, plant them direct in prepared soil.

Some herbs, such as mint, produce rhizomes – stems that run from the plant at ground level or under ground. Rhizomes produce both roots and shoots along their length that look like several separate plants but are, in fact, all connected. Divide rhizomes after flowering or in spring.

DROPPING

Dropping is a traditional method of propagating woody plants. It involves digging a hole deep enough to half-sink the plant in the soil. Where the stems touch the soil a new root system will be produced. Once established the new plants can be detached from the parent and planted in a different site.

1 In the spring dig a hole large enough to sink the plant up to about halfway along its stems.

2 Place the plant in the hole and carefully push the soil back around the stems.

3 Keep the plant watered during dry spells and lift in the autumn, when roots should have formed on the stems. Cut each one from the main plant and pot them up as individual cuttings.

Watering

Water is essential for all plant growth, although some plants have adapted to drought conditions and need very little moisture in order to survive. If you live in a climate with low rainfall it is important to choose plants that will tolerate dry conditions, unless you are able to spend time and thought on watering systems. Roof gardens and other sites exposed to drying winds increase the watering needs of your plants.

A variety of watering systems and devices are available to help you, notably drip-watering systems and water-retaining granules. It is best to water at dawn or dusk when the sun's rays are less powerful and the evaporation rate is much reduced. To encourage deep roots to develop, water thoroughly and regularly rather than little and more often, especially when watering lawns.

Easy-watering systems

In any garden, easy access to water is essential, as many plants will require regular watering. An outdoor tap is vital, unless the kitchen tap is easily accessible. Also essential is a hose that is long enough to reach the farthest corners of the garden.

In times of drought, however, water may be rationed and you may well have to recycle washing water from the house. Installing a water barrel to collect runoff rainwater is a sensible precaution.

There are some simple systems available which deliver water to the garden, as needed, at the flick of a switch. If you have a small garden in a warm climate, or if you garden on an exposed site, such as a roof terrace, consider planning a leaky pipe or drip-feed system, which can be laid permanently in the planting areas.

Drip-feed systems

This consists of a series of fine bore pipes, with drip heads at intervals, that you can position exactly where water is required – at the foot of plants needing

HOW TO WATER CONTAINERS

Plants in containers lose water very rapidly through evaporation. Terracotta pots especially are notoriously poor at retaining moisture. Hanging baskets, with their small amount of soil and large area exposed to the elements, are very greedy for water and may well need watering once a day in hot weather. Group containers together to preserve moisture, and put them in shade in hot weather.

Watering the root base
To make sure water penetrates the potting mix thoroughly, make a few holes around the edge of the pot with a cane before watering.

frequent watering, for example. A soil-moisture detector can be fitted to the system, ensuring that the automatic system is overridden if the ground is sufficiently damp. Drip-feed systems tend to get blocked with debris, so it is important to clean the system regularly.

Leaky-pipe hose system

This is useful for watering large areas, such as lawns, or for rows of vegetables. It is an efficient way of using water, because it is directed straight at the roots. The hose is punctured with a series of fine holes so that a regular, even supply of water is delivered over the length of the hose. A similar system uses a porous hose. The system can be buried beneath the soil to make it both permanent and unobtrusive.

Retaining moisture

A major difficulty with growing plants in containers is keeping the plants supplied with water, especially when using soilless potting compost, because these are very difficult to re-wet after drying out. To overcome this, add granules of polymer to the mix. When wetted, these granules swell to form a moisture-retaining gel which can hold vast amounts of water. The water is gradually released into the mix.

Making the most of water

There are various ways to reduce the need for watering. Firstly, you need to increase the moisture-retaining properties of the soil, if it is sandy, by adding plenty of organic matter. Secondly, you need to reduce the amount of water lost through evaporation, by screening your plants from the effects of drying winds.

Grouping plants together helps to reduce evaporation, as does using pebbles or stones over the soil surface.

Drought-resistant plants

Mediterranean herbs are excellent at surviving the droughts which they would find in their natural habitats. Choosing these plants will save a great deal of time and effort with watering. Generally speaking plants that are tolerant of drought can be recognized by their foliage. The leaves of drought-resistant plants are usually silver-grey, finely divided, and sometimes covered in fine hairs or felt – all of which reduce evaporation. Lavender and rosemary are good examples of these Mediterranean herbs.

Reviving a wilting plant
If a plant is wilting from lack of water, plunge it into a bowl of water so that the pot is covered. Leave it until air bubbles subside.

Watering hanging baskets
These types of containers dry out extremely quickly in summer. Soak the basket until the water drains from the bottom and all the compost is wet.

Feeding

In order to grow well, plants need a balanced diet of nutrients. Nitrogen, phosphorus and potassium are the foods plants must have in large amounts to sustain a good growth rate. Nitrogen is needed for healthy growth and leaves, phosphorus is essential for good root development and potassium ensures both healthy flowers and fruits as well as disease resistance.

As a gardener, you should supply your plants with these nutrients in various forms depending on the circumstances. Some forms are particularly useful for conditioning the soil, others for supplying a direct source of food to the plant itself. Quantities of nutrients required depend on how intensively the garden is cultivated: closely packed vegetables require a great deal; herbs much less. Fertilizers contain plant nutrients in a concentrated form and are used in fairly small quantities. Manures are bulky and need to be added to the soil in large amounts – but they provide only a small quantity of nutrients. However, they do add valuable fibre, which is converted into humus to condition the soil. This also increases the activity of beneficial microorganisms.

Composting animal manure
Animal manure is one of the best soil conditioners because it improves soil texture and provides some nutrients while the straw provides bulk. Compost manure for at least six months.

Fertilizers

These may be organic or inorganic in their origin. Organic fertilizers consist of dead plant or animal matter that has been processed, such as bonemeal, dried blood, and fishmeal. They do not scorch foliage and are natural products. Inorganic fertilizers, also known as artificial, chemical or synthetic fertilizers, are derived from mineral deposits or manufactured by an industrial process. These are highly concentrated and faster acting than organic types, but you must not exceed the dosage, or plants may be scorched or damaged.

Fertilizers can be applied in dried form or dissolved in water, as in liquid fertilizer.

Soil conditioners

Digging in quantities of bulky, organic matter introduces both nutrients and fibre into a garden soil.

Woody and fibrous material opens up heavy soils and improves the soil structure. It provides materials that improve moisture retention on lighter soils. Fibrous conditioners of this kind are ideal if long-term soil improvement is the ultimate aim. When they decompose they contribute to the formation of humus which absorbs other nutrients applied to the soil, apart from homemade garden compost and the different types of animal manures. Lime, while not a food, is also used to condition the soil. Never apply lime to the soil at the same time as fertilizers and manures.

Green manure

Organic matter can be added to the soil by growing a fast-maturing crop as temporary ground cover on a

APPLYING LIQUID FERTILIZERS

Liquid is usually easier and safer to apply than dry fertilizer, and the plant's response is often more rapid. The concentrated fertilizer is diluted in water. It is applied either to the soil or to the leaves (foliar feed), depending on the type. Mix the fertilizer thoroughly with the water before application, to reduce the chance of damaging the plants. Do not apply when rain is forecast, or it may be washed through the soil away from the plant's roots.

1 Dilute liquid fertilizers with water and apply with a watering can or a hose. These fast-acting fertilizers are useful for correcting nutritional deficiencies.

2 Apply liquid fertilizers as a foliar fertilizer or directly to the soil around the base of a plant. Most foliar fertilizers are soil-acting so runoff is absorbed by the roots.

bed that is empty for a while, usually over the winter. The crop is dug into the topsoil 6–8 weeks after germinating. This fast-maturing crop is known as a green manure and it is a means of improving both organic matter and nitrogen levels. The release of nitrogen is quite swift and so provides an early boost to plant growth. The greener and younger the manure, the less fibre is produced.

Dry fertilizers

These are nutrients in a dry, solid form – granules and pellets. They are mixed together and coated with a wax or resin compound which slowly dissolves and releases fertilizers into the soil. The release can take 6–18 months, depending on the thickness of the outer coating, soil moisture, temperature and pH. Apply these fertilizers by sprinkling them evenly over the soil and mixing them into the top layer with a fork. If the soil is dry, water the area after application to dissolve the fertilizer and wash it down to the root zone. An even distribution of fertilizer is essential, because damage to plants may occur if too much is used. Mark out the area you intend to fertilize into squares with canes and garden lines and then take care to sprinkle and spread the fertilizer as evenly as possible.

Fertilizing container-grown plants

To promote balanced and healthy growth in containers, use brand-name potting composts that contain measured amounts of fertilizer.

Additional fertilizers can be given if necessary by applying quick-acting fertilizers as a top-dressing, or by using foliar fertilizer or fertilizer spikes.

Mulching

A weed is any plant growing in a place where it is not wanted. Many weeds cause problems just because they are so tough and versatile that they can adapt to a wide range of growing conditions. For this reason they must always be dealt with before they get out of control. The most effective way to prevent them from appearing in the first place is to use a mulch.

Mulching for weed control

Mulching is the practice of covering the soil around plants with a layer of material to block out the light and help trap moisture. In today's gardens, where plastics are commonplace, inorganic black plastic sheeting is often chosen. Though not inviting to look at, it can be hidden beneath a thin layer of more attractive organic mulch.

As a general rule, organic mulches provide the bonus of improving the fertility of the soil, but inorganic mulches are more effective because they form a better weed barrier. To be fully effective as a barrier, organic mulches must be applied as a layer at least 10cm (4in) thick. Both organic and inorganic mulches tend to be less effective against established perennial weeds, unless an entire area can be sealed until the weeds have died out and planting is carried out through the mulch while it is in place. One way of clearing weedy ground in summer is to cover the soil with a mulch of clear or white plastic, sealed around the edges. Weeds are gradually killed by a combination of high temperatures and lack of carbon dioxide.

The plastic sheeting can be removed after a time and used elsewhere. The treated area is weed-free, ready to plant and cover with an organic mulch, such as shredded bark or gravel (see below).

Gravel mulch

Covering the soil with a mulch such as gravel will block out light and prevent weed seeds from germinating.

Weeding

Weeds compete directly with your garden plants for light, nutrients and water. They can also act as hosts to pests and diseases (see pages 48–9), which can spread as the season progresses. Groundsel, for instance, often harbours the fungal diseases rust and mildew, and sap-sucking aphids. Chickweed also plays host to aphids as well as red spider mites.

Perennial weeds

Digging up perennial weeds is an effective disposal system, provided that every bit of the root system is removed from the soil. If only a few weeds are present, try digging them out with a knife or trowel, but you must remove the top 5cm (2in) of root close to the surface, to prevent the weed from re-growing. This method can be used in the lawn to get rid of individual or small patches of weeds, and is a reliable means of eradicating weeds growing close to garden plants. In this situation, often no other weed control method would be effective without risking damage to plants growing nearby.

Clearing weeds

The simplest way to deal with weeds is to remove them physically, either by pulling or digging them out or, if they are small, hoeing them off at soil level.

The biggest problem with this method of control is that most weed seeds require exposure to light before they germinate. Often, when weeding disturbs the soil, more air is allowed into the surface layers and an ideal seedbed is created. Although the existing weed seedlings are destroyed, the weed growth cycle starts all over again. This problem is often worse when using rotovators, because they leave the surface layers of soil light and fluffy, making a perfect seedbed. Perennial weeds are increased, too, because they are chopped into pieces, each capable of growing.

The most effective way to clear weeds, especially established perennials, is to use a combination of cultural and chemical methods. Spray weeds in full growth with a chemical herbicide and, as they start to die, bury them when the area is dug over. When the new weed seedlings germinate, spray them with a chemical while they are most vulnerable.

Annual weeds

Clearing annual weeds with a hoe is quick and effective, but the timing is important. The hoeing must be done when the weeds are tiny and before they start producing seed.

Hoeing will sever the stems of young weeds from the root system just below soil level. This both prevents the stem from forming new roots and stops the roots from producing a new stem. When hoeing, make sure you always walk backwards to avoid treading weeds back into the soil.

There is an old saying, 'One year's seeds make seven years' weeds', which has now been endorsed by scientific research and proved to be remarkably accurate – unfortunately for gardeners.

Annual weeds are capable of producing a staggering total of 60,000 viable seeds per square yard, per year. The vast majority of these seeds are found in the uppermost 5cm (2in) of soil, but they will usually germinate only when exposed to sufficient light levels. This is why mulching (see opposite page), which covers the soil and blocks out light, has become such a widely popular method of weed control. The added benefit of mulching is that there is also little chance of contaminating the soil with chemical residue.

Herbs as companion plants

In the wild, you do not often see plants devastated by insect damage or demolished by armies of slugs and snails. Nature has its own balance of complementary plants and predators, which relies on a rich and varied but often crucial mixture of plants and wildlife. Here there is no monoculture – the kind of artificial environment we try and impose on our gardens.

If you are interested in gardening as organically as possible, you should explore the possibilities of companion planting: the pairing of herbs and wild plants with your hybridized flowers and vegetables, which will ultimately enrich the precious soil and not deplete it in the way that chemical control of pests and disease does.

Companion planting is believed to work through the scent of certain plants acting as a deterrent – which is why so many useful plants are herbal ones –

Companion planting
Interspersing plants like dill with crops will help to attract 'good' insects like hoverflies, which then attack aphids.

Companion herb plants

Herbs are not only beautiful – they are useful garden plants. Every plant in the garden affects the plants around it. It may be just by the large leaves offering shade and protection to more delicate plants. Some herbs deter pests and many attract beneficial insects that are valuable pollinators or act as predators of common garden pests.

The most common companion plant combinations are:

Borage, thyme and hyssop	attract bees which improve crop yield in strawberries and other fruit.
Chamomile	has been found to repel insect attacks, thus improving crop yields.
Chives	have a reputation for preventing black spot on leaves and deterring aphids.
Dill and fennel	attract hoverflies, which then go to work on aphids.
Garlic	with its strong odour is thought to be beneficial to roses.
Mint	especially the Pennyroyals have been found to be good fly and midge repellents.
Rosemary and thyme	mask the scent of carrots, which deters the carrot fly.
Sage	repels the cabbage white butterfly.
Nasturtium	has an excellent and interesting reputation as a companion plant. It keeps pests away from the vegetable garden, partly owing to the way it attracts aphids away from them. Nasturtium has also been found to repel ants and whitefly. It provides good ground cover and young leaves and flowers are delicious in salads.
Pot marigold	is a good all-round and attractive companion plant in the vegetable garden. It grows freely, is self-seeding and deters nematodes in the soil.

and through exudations of the roots, which alter the nutrient and bacterial make-up of the soil. For it to work effectively, you must introduce a carefully thought-out system of mixed planting that does not have regular beds separated by paths, but considers both the needs of individual plants and their effect on the soil by rotating crops not yearly, but as each comes into season. Thus, you might see strawberries interspersed with leeks, cauliflowers with celeriac or beetroot and lettuce.

General care and maintenance

Outlined below is a summary of the main points to bear in mind to help you grow and maintain healthy herbs through the season.

Sowing Sow seeds of annuals and perennials in spring. In milder climates, without deep winter frost, perennials can be sown in late summer or early autumn and will often overwinter as seedlings. Seeds that require stratification should be sown in later summer or autumn. Sow biennials in early summer to flower the following year (see pages 18–21).

Transplanting Transplant seedlings grown in trays once they are large enough to handle. Plant into individual pots and allow to establish. Harden off seedlings before planting into permanent sites (see pages 18–21).

Planting Water the plant well. Dig a hole more than large enough for its roots and deep enough to bring it to the same level in the ground as it was in the pot. Fill in the soil around the roots. Firm it down and water well (see pages 24–5).

Watering Water seedlings to keep them moist but do not overwater. Provide newly planted herbs with plenty of water until they are well established, particularly in dry weather. Water early in the day. Over or under watering will adversely affect your plants. If watering is necessary, soak the soil thoroughly to make sure moisture reaches the roots. Allow the soil to become dry before watering again.

Feeding Herbs that are planted into a well-prepared site should not need subsequent feeding except on poor soils for the first few years; incorporate garden compost or natural fertilizer into the soil beforehand. Mulch annually if necessary. Spray with a foliar feed if you suspect nutritional deficiencies (see pages 34–5).

Weeding Hoe or pull out weeds as they appear – avoid digging the soil, as this turns up new weed seeds and allows moisture to escape. Deeper rooting weeds need to be dug out individually or killed with a herbicide (see page 37).

Trimming After flowering and before the plant sets seed, trim with sharp secateurs or pruners to keep woody or herbaceous plants tidy. Cut back flowered stems to the main growth, leaving some stems for seed development if you want to collect seeds (see page 42–3).

Cutting back and pruning As growth starts in spring, remove up to three quarters of the previous season's growth on shrubby herbs that have become straggly or untidy. Do a light prune every year and a harder one every two or three years.

Controlling pests Early and regular control of common pests and diseases prevents them from causing widespread damage. Encourage natural predators and keep plants healthy with good gardening practice (see pages 48–9).

Harvesting Collect ripe seed, clean it and dry thoroughly before storing it clearly labelled in a cool, dry, dark place. Pick healthy foliage and flowers early in the day for drying, preserving in oil, or freezing (see pages 44–5).

Collecting seed

Herb seed heads can be used in winter arrangements, and their seed collected to produce new plants for the spring.

Seed collection

Collecting one's own seed is very satisfying and quickly becomes an obsession. The advantages of collecting your own seeds are many: fresh seed will be of the best quality, and you can select which plants to collect from.

It is usually obvious when seeds are ripe because the seeds or the seed capsules turn brown and dry. In order to collect seed, you should be familiar with the different types of seed heads and their methods of dispersal. The plant family often gives an indication of how the seed is held on the plant and how it is distributed. The families listed below are some of the most common, showing a variety of different seed heads and methods of collection. These methods can be applied to other plants that have similar seed heads:

- Borage family (Boraginaceae) Seeds resemble small black nuts that ripen over a long period of time, one at a time making collection difficult. Lay a sheet of muslin under the plant to collect the seed as it drops.
- Carrot family (Umbelliferae) Seeds are held on a flat head and will stay on the head for some time. Cut off the heads when ripe and shake or rub into a bag or bucket.
- Cranesbill family (Geraniaceae) A catapult mechanism ejects the ripe seeds. Seed heads must be collected just before ripening and kept in a bucket covered in muslin until seed is released.
- Daisy family (Compositae) Seeds are often held on an open head and frequently have a pappus or feathery hairs attached to aid dispersal by wind. Collect heads before seed disperses and shake off into a container.
- Pea family (Leguminosae) Many members of this family hold their round seeds in a pea-like pod. When the pod is dry and crisp (ripe), it splits and ejects the seeds. Collect pods when ripe but before they have opened.
- Poppy family (Papaveraceae) Poppies hold their tiny seeds in hard, often decorative, capsules at the top of the flower stem. When ripe the capsule develops small holes in the top and the seed will rattle inside. To collect just shake the seed into a container.
- Mint family (Labiatae) Seed is often dust-like and ripens all at once. Wait until the flower head turns brown and rub the head to see if the seed is ready to drop out.
- Primrose family (Primulaceae) Seed is held in a seed case and remains inside until ripe. When case is brown and ripe shake out the seed.

Cutting seed heads
Cut ripe seed heads just below the head and put into a paper bag. Some seeds disperse the moment they ripen; cut a long stem just before they are fully ripe, and hang up with a bag tied over the head to catch the seed.

Collected seed is often full of debris and, if small, needs to be cleaned (see pages 44–5). After cleaning, dry the seed on a tray or lid in a warm room for a few days. It is now ready for storing until it is needed. Put it in clearly labelled paper packets or envelopes. For short-term storage these can be kept somewhere dry and dark like a desk drawer or a biscuit tin, but they must be cool. For longer-term storage, over several years, seed can be kept in a sealed plastic container in the refrigerator (not the freezer). Seed for culinary use needs to be completely clean and free of debris.

RELEASING SEEDS

Many seeds can easily be released from their heads or capsules by simply shaking them out onto a flat surface like a tray or straight into a paper bag. Another method is to hang the seed heads upside down in a cool place and put a container underneath to catch them as they fall. Make sure the seed heads and the seeds remain dry at all times, as if they are put into storage while damp they will rot before they can be used.

Hard seed capsule
Poppy seed is produced in a rigid brown capsule that develops holes in the top when ripe. The thousands of tiny clean seeds can be shaken out.

Seed pod
The seeds of larkspur are held in an elongated pod that splits after ripening. Pick the ripened pods just before they open.

Soft seed capsule
Hollyhock seed is held in a hairy, brown, circular capsule that opens when the seed is ripe. The flat circular seeds drop out in great profusion.

Harvesting and storing

Herbs are versatile plants and have many practical applications. Both fresh and dried herbs are valued for their culinary and medicinal properties; dried herbs are a major ingredient of potpourri and make wonderful flower arrangements.

Drying

There are various methods of preserving herbs. For culinary or medicinal use, or for potpourri and dried flower arrangements, drying is often the most suitable method. Herbs that are dried correctly retain their flavour, colour and healing properties. Successful herb drying requires warmth, air flow and shade. Leaves of herbs can be picked for drying at any time. Harvest them when there is plentiful healthy foliage, preferably before the plant flowers, before the heat of the day but after the dew has dried. They are best left on the stalk. After harvesting, remove them from direct sunlight, as this bleaches them and evaporates the essential oils. Divide and tie the stems into small bunches to hang upside down in a warm, dark and airy place.

Other methods

Herbs that do not dry well, or lose their flavour when dried, are best frozen or preserved in oil. Especially recommended for freezing are basil, tarragon, fennel, chervil, parsley and chives; these can be stored in the freezer in sealed and labelled plastic bags. Chopped leaves and small flowers can also be preserved in ice cubes and look lovely if used in summer drinks.

CLEANING AND STORING SEEDS

If seeds are to be collected and stored for use next season, they need to be reasonably free of debris. Many seed heads, such as those of lavender below, are cut on their stems and are ready for cleaning.

1 Remove the dried heads from the stems. Pick out any stems, leaves and larger pieces of debris.

2 Rub the seed heads to make sure all the seeds have come out and then sieve through a fine mesh to clean the seed further.

Drying herbs Hang herbs in small bunches in a warm airy room, out of bright light. Hang bunches from a string suspended from the ceiling. When the leaves are crisp, rub them off the stalk and seal in a screw-top jar or store in a paper bag.

It is most important to make sure that the seed is absolutely dry before storing. **Warning:** Asthma sufferers and those sensitive to dust should not clean seed. For others a simple face mask can be worn to protect from dust.

3 Gently blowing the seeds will remove any remaining dust. The seeds are now ready for packing in a bag or envelope.

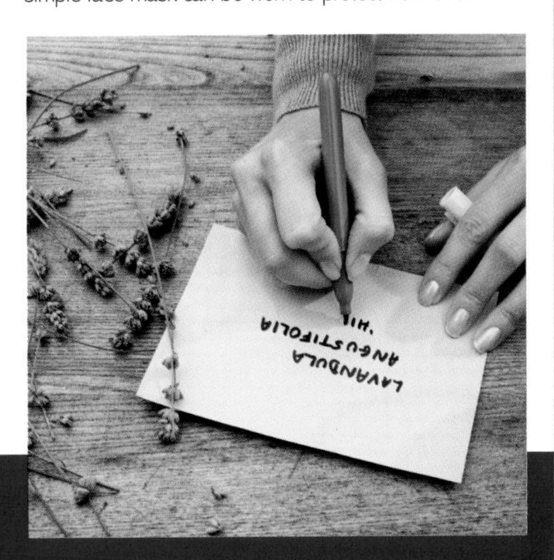

4 Label with the common name, the Latin name and the date and store in a cool, dark, dry place.

HERB PROPERTIES	Culinary	Medicinal	Scented	Flowering
Acanthus mollis (Acanthus)		•		•
Achillea millefolium (Yarrow)	•	•		•
Agastache foeniculum (Anise Hysop)	•	•	•	•
Ajuga reptans (Bugle)		•		•
Alchemilla vulgaris (Lady's Mantle)		•		•
Allium schoenoprasum (Chives)	•			•
Allium sativum (Garlic)	•	•		
Aloysia triphylla (Lemon Verbena)	•	•	•	•
Althaea officinalis (Marsh Mallow)	•	•		•
Althaea rosea (Hollyhock)		•		•
Anethum graveolens (Dill)	•			•
Angelica archangelica (Angelica)	•	•		•
Anthemis (Chamomile)		•	•	•
Anthriscus cerefolium (Chervil)	•			
Arctostaphylos uva-ursi (Bearberry)		•		•
Armoracia rusticana (Horseradish)	•	•		
Arnica montana (Arnica)		•		•
Artemisia dracunculus (French tarragon)	•		•	
Atriplex hortensis var. *rubra* (Red Orache)	•	•		
Borago officinalis (Borage)	•	•		•
Calamintha grandiflora (Garden Calamint)		•	•	•
Calendula officinalis (English Marigold, Pot Marigold)	•	•		•
Carum carvi (Caraway)	•			•
Chrysanthemum parthenium (Feverfew)		•		•
Cimicifuga racemosa (Black Cohosh)		•		•
Coriandrum sativum (Coriander)	•	•		•
Dictamnus purpureus (Burning Bush)	•		•	•
Digitalis (Foxglove)		•		•
Dipsacus fullonum (Teasel)			•	•
Echinacea purpurea (Purple Coneflower)		•		•
Eupatorium purpureum (Joe-pye Weed)		•		
Foeniculum vulgare 'Purpureum' (Bronze Fennel)		•		•
Galium odoratum (Sweet woodruff)		•	•	
Galium verum (Lady's Bedstraw)		•		•
Gentiana lutea (Yellow Gentian)		•		•
Hamamelis virginiana (Witch Hazel)		•		•
Helichrysum angustifolium (Curry Plant)			•	
Heliotropium arborescens (Heliotrope)			•	•
Hesperis matronalis (Sweet Rocket)	•		•	•
Humulus lupulus (Hop)	•	•		•
Hypericum perforatum (St John's Wort)		•		•

HERB PROPERTIES	Culinary	Medicinal	Scented	Flowering
Hyssopus (Hyssop)	•	•	•	•
Inula helenium (Elecampane)		•		•
Laurus nobilis (Sweet Bay)	•			
Lavandula (Lavender)		•	•	•
Levisticum officinale (Lovage)	•	•	•	•
Lobelia syphilitica (Great Lobelia)		•		•
Lythrum salicaria (Purple Loosestrife)		•		•
Marrubium vulgare (Horehound)		•		•
Melissa officinalis (Lemon Balm)	•		•	
Mentha (Mint)	•	•	•	•
Mentha x *piperita* (Peppermint)	•	•	•	•
Mentha pulegium (Pennyroyal)	•	•		•
Mentha spicata (Spearmint)	•	•	•	
Meum athamanticum (Spignel)	•			•
Monarda (Bergamot)	•		•	•
Myrrhis odorata (Sweet Cicely)	•	•		•
Nepeta mussinii (Catmint)	•	•	•	•
Nigella sativa (Fennel Flower)	•	•		•
Ocimum (Basil)	•		•	
Oenothera biennis (Evening Primrose)	•	•	•	•
Origanum (Oregano)	•	•	•	•
Perilla frutescens (Perilla)	•		•	
Petroselinum crispum (Parsley)	•	•		
Polemonium caeruleum (Jacob's Ladder)		•	•	•
Rosa (Rose)			•	•
Rosmarinus officinalis (Rosemary)	•	•		•
Ruta graveolens (Rue)		•	•	•
Salvia officinalis (Common Sage)	•	•		•
Sanguisorba minor (Salad Burnet)	•			
Santolina (Santolina)			•	•
Satureja hortensis (Summer Savory)	•	•		•
Satureja montana (Winter Savory)	•			
Scutellaria lateriflora (Skullcap)		•		•
Symphytum x *uplandicum* (Russian Comfrey)	•			•
Tanacetum balsamita (Costmary)		•	•	•
Tanacetum vulgare (Tansy)	•	•		•
Thymus vulgaris (Common Thyme)	•	•		•
Valeriana officinalis (Valerian)		•	•	•
Verbena (Vervain)		•		•
Viola odorata (Sweet Violet)	•	•	•	•
Viola tricolor (Heartsease)	•	•		•

Pests and diseases

These are the major pests, diseases and other problems that affect herbs. However, do not be alarmed, as although there are numerous things to be concerned about, your plants are unlikely to be troubled by all of these. For proven environmental reasons, there is a strong emphasis in these pages on non-chemical methods of control of the pests and diseases discussed.

Aphids

These are among the most troublesome of insect pests, particularly greenfly and blackfly, and they attack a wide range of flowers. Wash off aphids with plain or soapy water, or spray with insecticidal soap if necessary.

Black root rot

A disease affecting many flowers. The roots become black, but above-ground symptoms are yellowing and wilting leaves. Scrap sickly looking plants and plant something different in the affected site.

Bulb aphids

Certain aphids winter on bulbs and corms in store. Look out for them and simply rub them off.

Bulb rot

Bulbs of various kinds, such as alliums, are prone to rotting in store, caused by various diseases. Check for soft spots, particularly at the base of the bulbs (basal rot). Remove and discard rotting bulbs.

Caterpillars

The caterpillars of various moths and butterflies eat holes in the leaves of numerous perennials and annuals. They are generally green, brown or grey and are generally hairy. Caterpillars are easily picked off and destroyed, or plants can be sprayed with an insecticide if necessary.

Corm rot

Corms are prone to several kinds of rot while in store, so check regularly and remove and discard any that show signs of rot.

Cutworms

These caterpillars, the larvae of several different moths and greenish brown or greyish brown in colour, live in the soil and feed on roots and stem bases of plants, causing young plants to wilt and die. Remove any found during soil cultivations.

Damping off

This disease affects seedlings indoors, causing them to suddenly collapse and die. Damping off can spread rapidly and should be prevented by using sterilised compost and clean containers.

Earwigs

These night-feeding insects, easily recognised by their rear pincers, eat holes in flowers, buds and leaves. Remove and destroy any pests. Spray plants with an insecticide if necessary.

Foot rot

This disease causes the bases of stems to turn black and rot. Pull up and discard any plants that show signs of infection.

Grey mould

This major fungal disease, also known as botrytis, can infect all top growth of plants – flowers, buds, leaves and stems – resulting in rotting. Cut off any affected parts of plants, back to healthy tissue.

Leaf spot
Many diseases show up as brown or black spots on the leaves of numerous ornamental plants. The spots vary in size and some are in the form of rings. The best control method is to pick off any leaves showing spots. Spray affected plants with a fungicide if necessary.

Mildew
The most common is powdery mildew, appearing as white powdery patches on the leaves of many plants. Remove affected leaves. Spray plants with a fungicide if necessary.

Petal blight
This disease attacks some flowering herbs, showing as watery lesions or brown spots on the petals. Remove affected flowers. Spray plants with a fungicide if necessary.

Red spider mite
There are several kinds of these microscopic spider-like creatures that feed by sucking the sap from the leaves of many plants, particularly under glass. This results in fine pale yellow mottling on the upper leaf surfaces. Spraying plants regularly with plain water will deter the mites. Or spray plants with insecticidal soap if necessary.

Rhizome rot
This bacterial disease causes the leaves of rhizomatous herbs to turn yellow and wither. Dig up and discard badly affected plants. Avoid damaging surrounding plants as you do this.

Rust
This fungal disease shows as rust coloured, orange, yellow or dark brown raised spots on the leaves and stems. Affected leaves should be removed. Spray with a fungicide, if necessary.

Slugs and snails
Slugs and snails eat the leaves of a wide range of plants and also damage soft young stems and even flowers. Control by placing slug pellets around plants. Alternatively, remove them by hand.

Stem rot
Numerous diseases, but particularly sclerotinia, cause the stems of various perennials and annuals to rot. As there is no cure, plants that are badly affected should be removed and discarded.

Tuber rot
A fungal disease may attack tubers in store, causing them to rot. Check stored tubers regularly and if rotting is noticed cut it away to healthy tissue.

Viruses
Viruses are types of diseases that infect a wide range of plants. The most common symptoms are stunted and distorted plants. There is no cure: pull up and burn affected plants.

Weevils
These beetles are easily recognised by their elongated 'snout'. Their larvae are the main problem. Their feeding causes wilting, and invariably death in severe attacks. Use biological control with a pathogenic nematode in late summer.

Wilting leaves
Apart from wilting caused by various pests and diseases, the most common cause is drought. Young plants may never recover, even if watering is carried out. Make sure the soil never dries out, ideally by mulching permanent plants and by watering as necessary.

Woodlice
These pests feed at night and hide in dark places during the day. Physical control is not practical, except to ensure that any plant debris is not left lying around.

DIRECTORY

Aromatic Herbs

Aloysia triphylla

Lemon Verbena

Lemon verbena forms a woody shrub in its natural habitat, and is cultivated chiefly for the amazing lemon scent of its leaves.

In mild climates it can be grown outdoors in sheltered positions, on light, well-drained soil. As it is only half-hardy, it is normally best grown in a container. In winter, before any hard frosts, move the container indoors. The plant will be dormant over the winter and come into leaf in late spring. Cut it back to shape at this stage, and you will have a decorative and highly scented shrub to put out on the patio. Lemon verbena is prone to infestation by red spider mites. Use cold-water sprays or insecticidal soap to control them.

The leaves of lemon verbena make a delicious tea, which is soothing for digestion, and add a delightful lemon fragrance to many dishes. Always harvest the leaves before the plant flowers.

Care

Lemon verbena prefers rich, well-drained soil and a site in full sun.

New plants

Take semi-ripe cuttings in summer, kept under plastic or mist. The seeds of this plant are rarely obtainable.

Anthemis

Chamomile

With their small, white, daisylike flowers, all the chamomiles make attractive garden plants and form a decorative, creeping ground cover. The wonderful apple-scented foliage provides fragrant lawns. With a maximum height of 15cm (6in), the double cream form illustrated is a lovely low-growing plant for the rock garden, the front of a border, or a formal herb garden. A. nobile grows to 30 cm (12 in) high in flower and looks equally good in the border or herb garden. As a lawn herb it needs to be cut regularly, although the nonflowering clone, 'Treneague', requires no cutting. A. tinctoria, with larger, yellow flowers, is known as dyer's chamomile and produces bright yellow dyes. It grows 60cm (2ft) high, and the foliage is not apple-scented.

Chamomile, one of the oldest garden herbs, was revered by the ancient Egyptians for its curative powers. For centuries it has been grown in herb gardens both for decoration and for its medicinal properties.

Care

Chamomile prefers well drained, sandy soil and a site in full sun, although it will tolerate partial shade.

New plants

Sow seeds in spring in fine soil; divide plants in spring.

Artemisia

Artemisia

The genus Artemisia contains a wide range of silver-grey foliage plants and several aromatic herbs, including *A. absinthium* (wormwood), *A. abrotanum* (southernwood), *A. pontica* (Roman wormwood), and the indispensible culinary herb *A. dracunculus* (French tarragon). All these herbs, except the last, have particularly decorative leaves and, with their silver-grey colouring, are invaluable in mixed plantings.

Wormwood, or green ginger as it is also known, is an outstanding foliage herb, especially the variety 'Lambrook Silver', and is undemanding in its requirements.

Wormwood is a bitter herb and was used to make the lethal drink absinthe. The attractive green-grey foliage of southernwood has a fragrant fruity scent. Roman wormwood has finely divided and fragrant leaves. *A. ludoviciana* (western mugwort) is an exceptionally decorative plant.

Care

All varieties seem to thrive in drought conditions, but they do demand good winter drainage as they will not survive with waterlogged soil around their roots. The ground-cover varieties require a covering of grit or gravel, to keep wet soil off their foliage.

New plants

Sow seeds in late summer; take semi-ripe cuttings in summer; divide in autumn.

Calamintha grandiflora

Garden Calamint

Garden calamint, also known as mountain balm, is a small bushy plant with mint-scented leaves. The small, pink, sagelike flowers continue for a long season.

Grow calamint near the edge of the border, where its scent can be appreciated and its attractive flowers enjoyed. It looks good in the rock garden but needs to be out of the hottest sun in light or partial shade and can also be grown in the dappled shade of trees or on a hedge bank.

Garden calamint has some healing properties, although it cannot be considered an important medicinal plant. A tisane made from either fresh or dried leaves is refreshing and a mild tonic. John Gerard, the English herbalist, recommended calamint for the cure of melancholy, so this is a tea that could be a pleasant pick-me-up during the dull days of winter.

Care

Garden calamint will tolerate most soils if they are well drained. It requires a site in partial shade.

New plants

Sow seeds in spring; divide in autumn or spring; take cuttings in spring.

Dictamnus purpureus

Burning Bush

Burning bush is so called because the flowers give off an inflammable vapour in hot, dry conditions. The whole plant is also highly aromatic, reminiscent of lemon peel and balsam.

Burning bush is also sometimes known as white (or purple) dittany or fraxinella. It is not related to and should not be confused with the other dittany, *Origanum dictamnus* (Dittany of Crete), which is a member of the mint family.

Burning bush is a magnificent-looking plant that should have a lightly shaded position in a border, with a fairly dry loam soil. Grow it with other plants that enjoy similar conditions, such as *Filipendula vulgaris* (dropwort), *Linum perenne* (perennial flax), and *Pulsatilla vulgaris* (pasqueflower).

The plant has been used medicinally in the past but is little valued today. The scented leaves provide a tea substitute.

Care

Burning bush likes well-drained alkaline loam and a site in partial shade.

New plants

Sow seeds fresh in late summer; divide in spring; take root cuttings in late autumn or early winter.

H 60–90cm (24–30in)
S 45cm (18in)

15–17°C (60–62°F)

Partial shade

Helichrysum angustifolium

Curry Plant

The curry plant is a fairly recent introduction to the herb garden and something of a novelty. Brushing against this plant is an extraordinary experience as the aroma of curry is mysteriously released. This shrub retains its silver-grey foliage through the winter months, and is very drought resistant. The dwarf variety 'Nanum' is superb for the rock garden and makes a neat edging for a formal herb or knot garden.

The one vital growth requirement for curry plant is sharp drainage. It is pretty hardy, but will not survive wet, cold soil over winter. Clip it lightly after flowering and again in spring.

Although curry plant is not really a culinary herb, it can be used experimentally to give the subtlest curry flavour to soups, stews and vegetables.

Care

Curry plant prefers sharply drained and not too fertile soil. It requires a site in full sun.

New plants

Take soft or semiripe cuttings in spring and summer.

Heliotropium arborescens

Heliotrope

Heliotrope is so named because its flowers move with the sun. This is a beautifully scented plant, which bears dense clusters of vivid purple, sweetly fragrant flowers over a long period. The semiglossy foliage is an attractive burnished purple.

In warm frost-free climates, heliotrope grows into a small, bushy shrub. In areas with cold winters, it should be treated as an annual and either planted out after the danger of frost is over or grown in a container. It thrives in most good soils, but needs some moisture. Position it near the house, where its scent can be appreciated.

Heliotrope flowers are excellent in potpourri, and the herb was once used in homeopathic medicine.

Care

This plant prefers fertile, well-drained soil and a site in full sun.

New plants

Sow seeds in spring; take cuttings in summer. Germination of the seeds occurs at about 21°C (70°F) and takes approximately three weeks. Softwood cuttings can easily be taken, and this is often worth doing to maintain a plant with a particularly strong scent.

Hesperis matronalis

Sweet Rocket

Sweet rocket is also called dame's violet and vesper flower because the flowers emit their scent only after sunset. Do not confuse it with *Eruca sativa* (the annual, Mediterranean rocket, or arugula), a salad herb.

Sweet rocket is vigorous and can grow tall in the right conditions, so give it space. Plant it near the house so that its evening scent can be fully appreciated. The plant should be allowed to self-seed in a planting in sun or light shade. The lovely white form should always be grown in some shade; against a dark background it looks cool and striking.

The leaves of sweet rocket are used to add a bitter tang to green salads. Collect them before the plant flowers. Medicinally this herb is used as an antiscorbutic because it has a high vitamin C content.

Care

Sweet rocket prefers rich, moisture-retaining loam, but is tolerant of poor soil. It requires a site in full sun, but it will tolerate partial shade.

New plants

Sow seeds in spring or late summer; take basal cuttings in spring.

Lavandula

Lavender

Lavender, which must be among the most well known of all scented herbs, keeps its grey-green leaves over winter and flowers for many weeks. A huge number of species and varieties are available

Lavenders in great variety are ideal for edging and hedging. They can be kept neatly clipped after the flowers are over. If plants become too large, cutting back more severely in spring will improve them. For a tall hedge 'Old English' or 'Grappenhall' are the largest growing plants. There are several good, intermediate-size lavenders and a wide choice of dwarf lavenders from which to select your preferred flower and foliage colour.

Medicinally lavender is used as a mild sedative, an antiseptic, an antispasmodic and a carminative. The essential oil derived from lavender is one of the most valuable and has many applications.

Care

Grow in well-drained, alkaline soil which is not too rich. This plant needs full sun in order to thrive.

New plants

Sow seeds in autumn; take greenwood cuttings in spring, hardwood cuttings in summer or autumn.

Melissa officinalis

Lemon Balm

An easy and undemanding herb to grow, lemon balm will withstand considerable heat and drought, and will even flourish at the base of a sunny wall. It is not a particularly decorative plant, but if cut down after flowering it will remain neat and green, and will also produce more leaf for cutting. However, *M. officinalis* 'Aurea' (golden lemon balm) is worth growing for its pretty gold-and-green, variegated leaves, and the variety *M. officinalis* 'All Gold' is also highly recommended. These golden balms look and do best in a little shade; otherwise the leaves tend to brown.

The Arabs regard lemon balm as a valuable medicinal plant, with particular benefit for treating anxiety and depression and as a sedative and tonic tea. The ancient Greeks grew it as an important bee plant and for its scented foliage.

Care

Lemon balm enjoys fairly fertile, well-drained loam and a site in partial shade.

New plants

Divide roots or sow seeds in spring (germination can be erratic); take cuttings in spring and early summer.

Mentha

Mint

Mints worth growing are: *M. spicata* 'Moroccan', the best for mint sauce and mint drinks; *M.* x *piperita piperita* (peppermint), is also available with decorative crisped leaves; *M.* x *piperita* var. *citrata* (bergamot or eau de Cologne mint), with red-tinged, scented foliage; *M. suaveolens* (apple mint), and also its white-variegated form, *M. suaveolens* 'Variegata', often known as pineapple mint; and the vigorous, woolly leaved *M.* x *villosa alopecuroides* 'Bowles' (Bowles mint), which gives a superb flavour to mint sauce and new potatoes.

Mints require a rich, well-drained loam that will retain moisture in summer. If they are put under stress with too few nutrients or, more important, too little moisture, they become unhealthy and susceptible to rust and – in the case of woolly leaved mints – to mildew.

Mints, especially peppermint and spearmint, are valuable medicinally and make a delightful and soothing tea. Eau de Cologne or bergamot mint is used in perfumes and soaps.

Care

Mints like fertile, well-drained, moist loam and a site in full sun, although they will tolerate partial shade.

New plants

Divide runners in autumn; root cuttings in water or compost in spring and early summer.

Rosa

Rose

The rose is our most popular and best-loved garden plant. There are said to be over 10,000 cultivated varieties.

The rose is an extremely versatile plant: there is one for every garden. Most prefer a rich, fertile loam soil which is clay based and retains moisture. However, there are varieties that will grow in sandy or poor conditions, and many that will tolerate some shade. Many roses make excellent decorative hedges, but most are used in the garden as specimen shrubs, climbers, or ramblers. A mixed selection can also be planted into a specially prepared bed.

Today attar of roses is one of the most popular ingredients of perfume, soaps and cosmetics. Although the rose is now little used medicinally, the essential oil is valued in aromatherapy to treat many conditions. Rose hips are extensively used as a rich source of vitamin C. Rose petals are indispensable in potpourri; they retain their fragrance for a long period and also keep their colour well when dried.

Care

Roses are tolerant of soil type but do best in clay-based loam. They prefer a site in full sun or partial shade.

New plants

Sow seeds of species in autumn (stratify); try layering in mid-summer; take cuttings of current year's growth in early autumn.

Santolina

Santolina

Santolina, or cotton lavender, looks nothing like lavender and is in no way related to it. However, its finely cut foliage is just as decorative and as useful in the herb garden.

Santolina grows naturally on dry, stony soils which are baked by the hot Mediterranean sun, so this is a plant that will survive heat and dry soil conditions.

There is a good variety of santolinas available for the garden, each with its own distinctive texture, such as *S. chamaecyparissus* 'Lemon Queen'. This has lovely, soft lemon-coloured flowers and a low spreading habit, which provides excellent ground cover in dry stony areas; it is a decorative rock garden plant. Santolina makes a superb hedge, especially the compact form: it can be kept tightly clipped and shaped and looks good all year round.

The shrub was used medicinally but nowadays is more valued for decorative use, in both fresh and dried forms, and as an insect repellent.

Care

Santolina prefers well-drained, alkaline soil, dry in summer. It requires a site in full sun.

New plants

Take tip cuttings in spring or summer.

H To 60cm (24in) S 45cm (18in)

15–17°C (60–62°F)

Direct sunlight

Viola odorata

Sweet Violet

This lovely herb has always been the harbinger of spring. Every garden, however small it is, should have sweet violets growing in some shady corner, perhaps around a tree, among shrubs, or at the edge of woodland where there is shade during the hottest part of the day. Violets will also establish themselves in short grass. They need some moisture and enjoy a woodland-type soil with plenty of leaf mould. A few plants will soon spread in suitable conditions. Sweet violets look best growing with other wild woodland herbs, such as primroses, oxlips, hellebores, wild strawberries and lungwort. Grow violets in earthenware containers, which can be brought into the house in winter and placed on a windowsill.

Medicinally sweet violet is valued for its soothing expectorant properties in the treatment of respiratory disorders, including bronchitis. It alleviates and cools hot swellings, and is also mildly sedative. The flowers are extensively used in perfumery. In Britain the flowers were cooked with meat and game and can be candied.

Care

Violets like moisture-retaining to moist, humus-rich, alkaline soil and a site in partial shade.

New plants

Sow seeds in autumn; divide in late winter or early spring.

DIRECTORY

Culinary Herbs

Allium schoenoprasum

Chives

Chives have particularly pretty, pink to purple flower heads and make a lovely edging for a border or formal herb garden. Even when not in flower, the clumps of lush green, cylindrical, hollow stems are attractive.

Chives prefer a fertile soil with some moisture, but will grow in surprisingly dry conditions, including gravel or the rock garden. To propagate divide into clumps of half a dozen small bulbs and replant during the spring. Chives die down completely in winter.

Chives have become a popular and indispensable seasoning, imparting a delicate onion flavour. The flowers can be used to decorate and flavour salads and soups.

Care

Chives prefer moist rich loam in direct sunlight.

New plants

Sow in seed trays indoors in spring and then plant out in groups of three or four seedlings. Established groups can be divided every three or four years in spring or autumn.

Allium sativum

Garlic

Common garlic can be classed either as a herb or a vegetable. It is a close relation of the onion, and its growth habit and appearance are similar. Garlic is probably the most commonly used herb in the kitchen. Many famous dishes are based on garlic, such as *aïoli*, a garlicky mayonnaise dip from Provence. Garlic is also much valued in herbal medicine, as a digestive and in the treatment of high blood pressure. It is also supposed to ward off the common cold.

Care

Garlic prefers fertile, sandy to moist loam and a site in full sun, although it will tolerate partial shade.

New plants

Plant individual cloves in the autumn approximately 10cm (4in) deep and 18cm (7in) apart; most varieties need at least two months at temperatures between 0–10°C (32–50°F). Do not plant on ground that has been recently manured.

Anethum graveolens

Dill

All forms of dill are decorative at every stage of growth. With its feathery foliage, dill looks pretty in a border or in a formal herb garden and produces attractive flower and seed heads, which dry well.

Dill should be grown in a clump or mass. Sow it in spring by broadcasting the seeds. In order to obtain a good leaf harvest use the most suitable variety (listed below), and make sure that the plants do not dry out, as they will go straight up to flower.

Dill has always been an essential flavouring in Scandinavian cooking where it is used in pickling and fish dishes, most famously in gravadlax, salmon pickled with dill. The seeds are used extensively for pickling cucumbers and to flavour bread and cakes. The chopped leaves are sprinkled on many dishes. Dill seed is good for the digestion.

Care

Dill tolerates most soils and resists drought. It prefers a site in full sun.

New plants

Sow seeds in spring, or plant in succession for culinary use.

Angelica archangelica

Angelica

The stately angelica is a striking plant by any standards. It should be grown for its decorative and architectural value as a specimen. Plant either near water or in a mixed border. In the first year angelica normally produces only a large leafy rosette. It will self-seed profusely.

Angelica stem is used as a green candied cake decoration. The herb is also an ingredient of certain liqueurs, such as Benedictine. Medicinally it is used as an infusion to treat bronchitis, flatulence and colds. Angelica can be mistaken in the wild for water hemlock which is very poisonous and favours a similar habitat.

Care

Angelica likes soil that is rich, deep and moist, either in full sunlight or light shade.

New plants

Sow fresh seeds where you wish the plants to grow, in the autumn. Transplant these to 90cm (36in) during the spring.

Anthriscus cerefolium

Chervil

An attractive herb with extremely delicate, fern-like leaves and pretty white flowers, chervil is very short lived in many situations and goes rapidly to seed. However, the seedlings make a fine ground cover.

Chervil does best in cool, slightly moist conditions. Grow it where it will receive sun in winter but will be shaded as the sun heats up. It is best sown in late summer for a winter and spring crop, and again in early spring to produce leaf in early summer.

As a culinary herb chervil should be more widely used. In France it is appreciated as an ingredient of *fines herbes* and *bouquet garni*. The flavour is very delicate, with a hint of aniseed. It is used to flavour soups and stews and should be added at the last minute as otherwise the flavour will be lost in cooking.

Care

Chervil prefers light soil with humus and some moisture. It requires a site which is partially shady in summer.

New plants

Sow seed in spring and late summer where the plants are to grow. Thin plants to 15cm (6in) apart and water regularly during the summer. Seed sown in early spring will mature in the summer. Seed sown in late summer will produce leaves over the winter.

Armoracia rusticana

Horseradish

Horseradish is a perennial plant of the Brassicaceae family, which also includes mustard, wasabi, broccoli and cabbages. The plant is probably native to southeastern Europe and western Asia, but is popular around the world today. It grows up to 1.5m (5ft) tall and is mainly cultivated for its large white, tapered root.

The intact horseradish root has hardly any aroma. When cut or grated, however, enzymes from the damaged plant cells break down and produce mustard oil, which irritates the sinuses and eyes. Once grated, if not used immediately or mixed in vinegar, the root darkens and loses its pungency and becomes unpleasantly bitter when exposed to air and heat.

Horseradish has been cultivated since antiquity. Both root and leaves were used as a medicine during the Middle Ages and the root was used as a condiment on meats in Germany, Scandinavia and Britain.

Care

Horseradish likes a moist, neutral soil in direct sunlight, although it will tolerate partial shade.

New plants

Propagate by dividing rhizomes, tubers, corms or bulbs (including offsets).

Artemisia dracunculus

French tarragon

This herbaceous perennial is much used in the kitchen, particularly to flavour vinegar, and was historically used to cure toothache. The leaves are also used in salads and as a seasoning. Grown as a kitchen herb, the leaves can be cut and used when young. Alternatively, cut off the flower heads as they form and then cut and dry the stems for use during the autumn and winter. Strip the leaves from the plant when drying is complete and store them in airtight bottles. French tarragon is not totally hardy and protection may be needed in hard winters in cold districts.

Care

French tarragon prefers fertile soil mixed with crushed rocks, sand and gravel for good drainage. It requires a site in full sun and the base of the plant must not be shaded.

New plants

Sow seeds in late summer; take semiripe cuttings in summer; divide in the autumn.

Warning Other types of Artemisia are potentially toxic; only use *A. dracunculus* or *A. d. dracunculoides* (Russian tarragon).

Borago officinalis

Borage

Borage, or burrage, has long been grown in herb gardens and is a firm favourite because of its beautiful intense blue, starlike flowers.

Borage self-seeds readily and in good soil forms a substantial plant. If you keep bees, it is worth seeding a large patch since it will flower for months and bees love it. Borage will grow well in a container of rich soil, but will need frequent watering in hot weather. It self-seeds readily.

Borage leaves impart a fresh cucumber flavour to summer drinks and should be used in fruit cups and wine cups. The young leaves make a delicious addition to a green salad, and the flowers look spectacular sprinkled over the top. The flowers can also be candied. Wonderful honey is produced from the flowers. Traditionally borage was used to drive away sorrow and melancholy. It has well-tried medicinal properties and an infusion makes a soothing treatment for bronchitis and catarrh.

Care

Borage can be planted in most well-drained soils and thrives in full sun, although it will tolerate partial shade.

New plants

Sow the seeds in spring. Divide in the autumn or spring and take cuttings in the spring.

Carum carvi

Caraway

Caraway is closely related to dill, fennel, anise and cumin. The dainty white flower heads are set off well by its finely cut, fernlike foliage which creates a wonderfully soft texture when grown in a clump. Sown in summer, the small plants will establish before the winter and make an attractive ground cover. They will mature the following summer. Gather seeds when they are brown and ripe.

Caraway, mentioned in the Bible and grown by the ancient Egyptians, has been in use for 5,000 years. The young leaves can be added to salads, and the root cooked as a vegetable. The seeds are extensively utilized to flavour cakes and breads, and to season vegetables, cheese and sausages. The seeds have also long been utilized medicinally, in particular to soothe digestive upsets.

Care

Caraway will grow happily in most soils, especially light ones. It prefers a site in full sun.

New plants

Sow seeds in late summer *in situ*. Thin to 15cm (6in) apart. The plant will carry flower heads and seeds in its second year.

Coriandrum sativum

Coriander

Coriander is an ancient herb and spice used for over 3,000 years. An extremely beautiful plant when in flower and seed, it has decorative, glossy, bright green leaves and pretty white flowers with a pink-mauve tinge. In the herb garden coriander looks delightful, and it can also be grown in gravel, provided that there is some moisture.

Sow the large seeds from spring to summer about 1cm (½in) deep. For maximum leaf harvest choose a variety specifically for leaf production and make sure that the soil is fertile and well drained; for good supplies of leaf, sow the seeds in succession.

Both coriander seeds and the fresh leaf are used extensively to flavour cakes, curries, Frankfurters, various liqueurs, pastries, bread and sweets. The seeds help to aid digestion.

Care

Coriander will grow successfully in any fertile well-drained soil. It prefers a site in full sun.

New plants

Sow seed in spring and early summer and thin to 15cm (6in) apart.

Foeniculum vulgare 'Purpureum'

Bronze Fennel

Fennel provides feathery spring foliage, and looks superb in almost any garden setting. The bronze variety is particularly handsome. The attractive yellow flower heads are visited by bees and other insects. Its main requirement is a hot, sunny situation and very well-drained soil.

The whole plant has an aniseed flavour, and is indispensable in many dishes, especially fish. The seeds are used to sprinkle on sweets, cakes and breads. The thick bulbous stem of the sweet, or Florence, fennel (*F. v.* var. *azoricum*) is eaten as a vegetable. Both the seeds and root of fennel are valued medicinally for their digestive properties. The tops yield bronze-green and brown dyes.

Care

This plant requires well-drained deep soil and prefers a site in full sun.

New plants

Sow seeds in autumn or spring.

Hyssopus

Hyssop

Hyssop is an ancient herb mentioned in the Bible. It forms a woody, neat, upright shurb. When in bloom the intense blue flowers are a glorious sight. Hyssop can be planted as a hedge or decorative border; keep it well trimmed. It looks particularly good with the lax-growing, grey-leaved catmint. If using different colours of hyssop, grow a predominance of one shade with a small proportion of other colours interspersed. Hyssop also makes an attractive specimen plant in the herb garden, and is an excellent bee and butterfly plant. *H.aristatus*, the smaller-growing mountain hyssop, which has deep blue flowers in late summer (after *H.officinalis*), is a good rock plant; its leaves are a brighter green.

Hyssop is traditionally used in liqueurs like Benedictine and Chartreuse. In times gone by it was employed as a stewing herb because of its strong scent and curative virtues. Medicinally hyssop is valuable taken as an infusion to treat colds, bronchitis, sore throats and catarrh.

Care

Hyssop thrives in well-drained and rather light soil and prefers a site that is in full sun.

New plants

Sow Hyssop seeds in the spring or late summer and take cuttings in late spring or early summer.

Laurus nobilis

Sweet Bay

The sweet bay, or sweet laurel, is one of the best-known aromatic, evergreen trees. Now grown mainly for its culinary virtues, it was once a sacred tree to the Greeks and Romans; the leaves were traditionally used to crown returning victors from the wars in Ancient Rome.

Bay should be grown in a sheltered spot protected from icy winds which will burn its leaves and even cut it to the ground in harsh weather. It enjoys the partial shade of other trees. In areas of deep winter cold, grow bay in a container, and bring it inside during hard weather. It can be clipped to various shapes and cut back hard in late summer. Bay trees have smooth pointed leaves that are dried and used to flavour stews.

Care

Bay will tolerate most well-drained, moisture-retaining, fertile soils. It prefers a sheltered site in full sun, although it will tolerate partial shade.

New plants

Bay is not an easy herb to propagate; buying a small plant is the best way to get started. Alternatively, Sow fresh, moist seed in autumn; take semi-ripe cuttings in late summer, best using mist and bottom heat.

Levisticum officinale

Lovage

A large and leafy herb, lovage was a popular medicinal in the Middle Ages, when it was grown by the Benedictine monks. The ancient Greeks also valued it and chewed the small aromatic leaves to help relieve indigestion. The distinctive scent is close to that of celery.

In a rich soil lovage can grow to massive proportions after a few years. One plant only is required in the garden; give it ample space in full sun. When the flowers are over, cut the stems down to stop the plant from falling over and self-seeding.

Lovage, formerly believed to be an aphrodisiac, was used in love potions. In the kitchen, it is invaluable if used sparingly, giving a celery flavour to many dishes. The chopped leaves and young stems can be added to salads, and the seeds and leaves make a tea that is helpful in the treatment of indigestion and flatulence.

Care

Lovage prefers a rich, deep, moisture-retaining but well-drained soil. It requires a site in full sun.

New plants

Sow seeds in autumn (when ripe) or spring; divide plants in early spring.

Mentha pulegium

Pennyroyal

Pennyroyal is a plant in the mint genus, within the family Lamiaceae. Crushed Pennyroyal leaves exhibit a very strong fragrance similar to spearmint. Pennyroyal is a traditional culinary herb and folk remedy. The essential oil of pennyroyal is used in aromatherapy, and is also high in pulegone, a highly toxic volatile organic compound affecting liver and uterine function.

Pennyroyal was commonly used as a cooking herb by the Greeks and Romans. The ancient Greeks often flavoured their wine with pennyroyal. A large number of the recipes in the Roman cookbook of Apicius call for the use of pennyroyal, often along with such herbs as lovage, oregano and coriander. Although still commonly used for cooking in the Middle Ages, it gradually fell out of use as a culinary herb and is seldom used so today.

Care

Mints like fertile, moisture-retentive soils and a site in full sun, although it will tolerate partial shade.

New plants

By division in autumn or spring.

Mentha spicata

Spearmint

The most commonly grown garden mint that is considered by many as the best for making mint sauce and for flavouring mint drinks in summer. Other favoured perennial mints in the kitchen are *M. suavolens*, (apple mint) or its variety *M. s.* 'Variegata' that has attractive white and green leaves and *M.* x *villosa alopecuroides* Bowles' Mint, a popular mint particularly used for flavouring new potatoes. Mints, especially peppermint and spearmint, are valuable medicinal and make a delightful and soothing tea. Eau de Cologne or bergamot mint is used in perfumes and soaps. In the home, mints have many applications: for instance, both peppermint and spearmint make refreshing additives to the bath.

Care

Mints like fertile, moisture-retentive soils and a site in full sun, although it will tolerate partial shade.

New plants

By division in autumn or spring.

Meum athamanticum

Spignel

Another name for this perennial herb is Baldmoney and it belongs to the parsnip family. The leaves are used in salads and other dishes as flavouring and the roots were formerly eaten as a vegetable. It is a popular herb in Scandinavian countries where it is called *bjørnerot*, or bear root, and dedicated to the Norse god Balder, god of the summer sun. The flavour is slightly reminiscent of curry. Grown in a container it requires a good depth of soil, although the roots will not reach their full depth for two or three years. It is an attractive plant and looks well in a container of herbs or in a rock garden.

Care

Spignel prefers sandy loam. This plant will not tolerate limy soil. It requires a site in full sun, although it will tolerate partial shade.

New plants

Sow seeds *in situ* in spring and thin to 15cm (6in) apart. Divide mature plants in spring.

Myrrhis odorata

Sweet Cicely

Sweet Cicely, with its soft green, fern-like leaves and white flower heads, is a lovely herb for the wild or woodland-edge garden. It has an aniseed scent. The masses of large shiny seeds become a rich brown colour as they ripen. After seeding it can be cut down and within a few weeks will grow fresh foliage.

All parts of the plant are edible. The leaves can be added to salads and take the tartness from cooked fruit. The white, fibrous roots may be eaten raw or boiled. The ripe seeds were also traditionally ground to give a perfume to furniture polish.

Sweet cicely was once valued for medicinal purposes, the leaves as a sugar substitute for diabetics, for the treatment of coughs and flatulence, and as a gentle stimulant. One of the original 'pot' herbs, it was also used in healing ointments for ulcers and as a tonic or gentle laxative. It was a sovereign remedy in cases of stomach trouble. The roots of this plant are antiseptic.

Care

Sweet cicely needs rich, moist to moisture-retaining loam in order to thrive and a site in full sun, although it will tolerate partial shade.

New plants

Sow seeds in autumn (stratify); divide in spring.

Nigella sativa

Fennel Flower

Fennel flower, or nutmeg flower, is a decorative annual herb closely related to *N. damascena* (love-in-a-mist), but bears paler blue to nearly white flowers. The blooms have a fascinating construction: the globular, horned seed pods are carried above the flowers. The herb is in no way related to fennel.

Fennel flower looks best when grown in a patch or drift, possibly in a rock garden or in an open border. In early spring the seedlings make a brilliant, light green carpet. It self-seeds profusely.

The Romans used the black seeds in cooking. The aromatic nutmeg-scented seeds are valued today as a seasoning in curries and many other dishes, for spreading on bread or cakes, and as a substitute for pepper. The seeds also have some medicinal properties and were employed to treat indigestion. The dried seed heads are highly decorative.

Care

Fennel flower will grow happily in any well-drained soil. It requires an open and sunny site.

New plants

Sow seeds *in situ* in spring or autumn. Some protection should be given for autumn-sown varieties.

Ocimum

Basil

Sweet basil was brought to Europe from India in the 16th century and has become one of the most popular culinary herbs. There are a number of varieties with different-coloured leaves from dark red to light green.

Sweet basil has a strongly aromatic, clovelike scent and is used extensively in the kitchen to season tomatoes, salads, vegetables, poultry and fish, and to make Italian pesto sauce. The leaves are best fresh, but may be dried or, better still, preserved in olive oil or as a frozen paste.

All varieties and species of basil are decorative, particularly those with purple or ruffled foliage, and they provide an attractive range of leaf and flower. Their distinctive scents are an added bonus. Many can be used as decorative edgings, especially the miniature Greek bush basil. Grow basil in small troughs or pots indoors, on the windowsill, or outside during the summer either in the soil or in containers.

Care

Basil prefers rich, well-drained, moisture-retentive soil and a sunny, sheltered site.

New plants

Sow seed at 13°C (55°F) in spring or *in situ* in summer.

Origanum

Oregano

A favourite perennial Mediterranean herb used to flavour stews and many pasta dishes, oregano is a bushy rhizomatous perennial that carries many flowers on upright stalks. These are most attractive to bees and insects and emerge pinkish-white from deep red bracts, although there are a number of naturally occurring colour variations.

The herbs mainly used for culinary purposes are: *O. onites* (often called pot marjoram), although it is not easy to obtain; *O. hirtum* (Greek marjoram or oregano), which has a fiery hot taste; *O. majorana* (sweet marjoram); and *O. vulgare* (wild marjoram or oregano).

Care

Oregano likes a nutrient rich, well-drained to dry, calcareous soil and a site in full sun. Cut back the stems of oregano after flowering to leave an attractive leafy mound until the herb grows up again in the following spring.

New plants

Sow seeds in spring; take cuttings in early summer. This plant self-seeds.

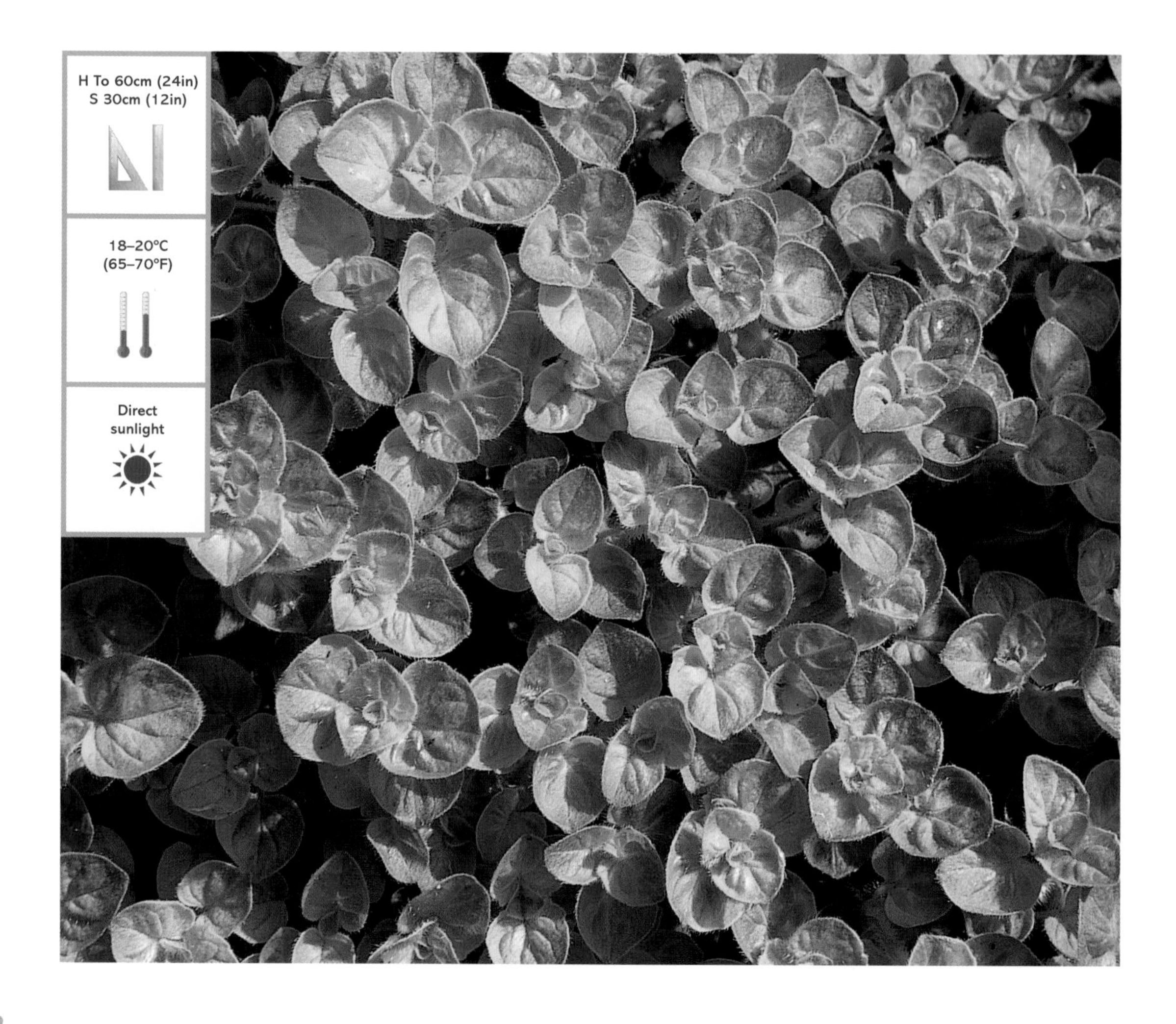

Perilla frutescens

Perilla

This colourful annual is valued in bedding schemes for its beautiful purple-bronze foliage. Perilla adds a splash of rich colour to any planting and is beautifully set off by some of the soft green and silver herbs. It can be used as a colourful edging in the formal garden and is invaluable in the potager. Plant it in bold groups to give dramatic colour and accent.

Used extensively in Japan, where it is known as shiso: the cinnamon-scented leaves provide a flavouring; the green variety is popular for sushi and tempura; the purple form is favoured for pickling, as it imparts its colour to the liquid. Use also in salads, soups and with vegetables. The leaves have an added hint of curry.

Care

Perilla prefers rich, moisture-retaining loam. It requires a site in partial shade.

New plants

Pre-chill seed in moist sand at 5°C (40°F) for three days (leave seed uncovered), then sow seeds in spring at 21°–27°C (70°–80°F).

Petroselinum crispum

Parsley

Parsley is a biennial often grown as an annual. It is one of the best-known herbs in the kitchen and is sprinkled over vegetables as a garnish and added to soups and stews. Parsley sauce is a traditional accompaniment for fish dishes. Parsley is rich in vitamin C and is used in the treatment of urinary disorders. It makes an excellent edge in a container of herbs. There are a number of varieties available. The flat-leaved parsley or French parsley is hardier than the curly-leaved varieties and has a stronger flavour. *P. tuberosum*, turnip-rooted or Hamburg parsley, has a large root that can be cooked or eaten raw.

Care

Parsley grows best in fertile, moisture-retentive soil and a site in full sun, although it will tolerate partial shade.

New plants

Sow seed in summer. It is difficult to germinate and requires a high temperature. It helps to soak the seed in warm water overnight and pour boiling water down the seed drills. It needs to be sown *in situ* as it resents being disturbed.

Rosmarinus officinalis

Rosemary

Rosemary has been used in the home since Roman times and old herbals tell of the many properties of the plant. It is the herb of remembrance and friendship and is supposed to stimulate the mind. An evergreen shrub, it can be grown easily in any container herb garden given a sheltered position, for although it comes from the Mediterranean it will tolerate some degree of frost. It flowers early in the year at the end of winter. In the kitchen it is the traditional accompaniment for roast lamb and can be used to flavour a number of other dishes. It is a slightly untidy plant, although some varieties are more compact than others, but it will not regenerate from old wood so care must be taken when trimming it back.

Rosemary is also extensively used in the cosmetics industry. Fresh or dried rosemary has some insect-repellent properties and is a natural antioxidant. Medicinally rosemary has diverse properties and is valued especially for the treatment of headaches, poor circulation, digestion and as a hair tonic.

Care

Rosemary prefers well-drained poor soil containing some lime. It likes a sheltered and sunny location.

New plants

Take semi-ripe cuttings or layer in summer.

Salvia officinalis

Common Sage

Salvias are a large group of plants including annuals, biennials, perennials and shrubs that are found in many gardens. Some are hardy, others that come from the tropics are greenhouse plants. The common sage, *Salvia officinalis*, and its varieties has been the best culinary herb for centuries and was formerly used in herbal medicine to treat depression, liver disorders, sore throats and mouth ulcers. An evergreen perennial or sub-shrub the leaves are often dried and stored for use and it is the main ingredient in sage and onion stuffing, a traditional accompaniment for roast poultry. It is also used to flavour fish, meat and cheese dishes.

Care

Sage prefers a well-drained, sandy loam and thrives in an open, sunny site. These herbs grow naturally in hot, dry, harsh conditions and must have good drainage if they are to survive hard, wet winters. They also require plenty of space and good air circulation to keep them dry at the base. Cut the plants back lightly after flowering and, if more drastic action is needed, cut harder back in spring.

New plants

Sow seeds in a cold frame in spring; take semi-ripe cuttings in summer.

Sanguisorba minor

Salad Burnet

A medieval 'pot' herb much used in the kitchen to flavour soups, sauces and cheese, and whose leaves were also eaten raw in salads. Medicinally the leaves were dried and used as a tea to cure digestive disorders and to treat diarrhoea and haemorrhages. The roots, also used as a decoction for burns, make a black dye used in tanning. *P. sanguisorba* is a clump-forming perennial and if grown in a container has to be divided every two or three years to keep the plant within bounds. Herbaceous burnets such as *S. canadensis*, Canadian burnet, and *S. officinalis*, greater burnet, have large bottlebrush flowers on terminal spikes.

Care

Salad Burnet prefers poor, chalky soil and a sunny site.

New plants

Sow seed *in situ* in spring. Divide plants in spring.

Satureja hortensis

Summer Savory

There are two sorts of savory. Winter savory is a foliage plant ideal for a low-growing container and often used to flavour beans. Summer savory is an annual, that can be grown to fill any bare areas. Sow seed *in situ* in spring. The hairy erect stems have small white flowers on spikes in the summer. If they are grown for use in the kitchen the plants should be pulled up and allowed to dry naturally and then the leaves should be picked off and stored. The flavour is slightly reminiscent of thyme and it can be used sparingly in a number of meat dishes and stuffings. A tea made from the leaves acts as a tonic and flowering shoots will repel moths when used in clothes.

Care

Summer Savory prefers well-drained, sandy loam.
It requires an open, sunny site.

New plants

Sow seeds *in situ* in spring when the soil has warmed up.

Satureja montana

Winter Savory

Winter savory has been used as a culinary herb since the 9th century. This is a decorative foliage plant, ideal for growing in the rock garden or gravel. The more delicate, creeping variety will tumble over rocks and spread over gravel. As a native of mountain regions, it will survive cold winters only if it is given sharp drainage and rather poor soil.

Winter savory is the perfect flavouring for beans. The annual *S. hortensis*, summer savory, with its thyme-like flavour, is used in many dishes and is easily grown from seed sown *in situ* in late spring. Make use of gaps between the shrubby herbs.

Care

Winter savory likes well-drained to dry, alkaline or sandy loam and a site in full sun.

New plants

Surface sow seeds in autumn (germination can be erratic); take semi-ripe cuttings in early summer.

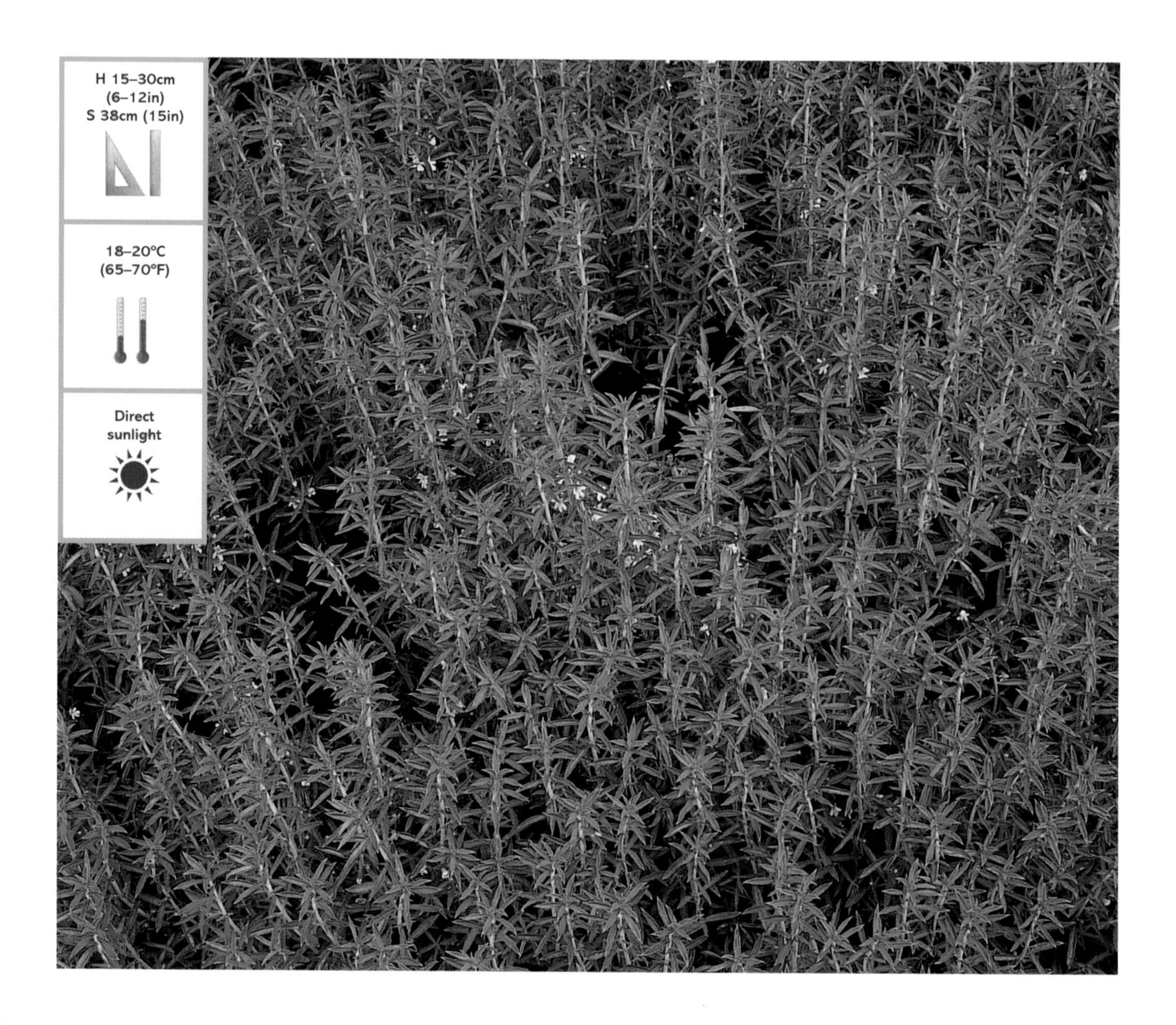

Tanacetum vulgare

Tansy

Crisp or fern-leaved tansy, an old cottage-garden herb, is one of the best herbaceous foliage plants. Allow tansy to form clumps in the border or woodland edge. It withstands periods of drought and dislikes wet soils. Cut the plant down to the base when the leaves lose their freshness.

Tansy has long been valued as an insecticide; it was used as a strewing herb. It is valued medicinally for expelling intestinal worms and to treat scabies. In Britain, tansy cakes and pudding were traditional at Easter.

The flowers and leaves yield yellow and green dyes for wool.

Care

Tansy prefers soil that is sharply drained and alkaline and a site that is in full sun.

New plants

Divide in the autumn, take cuttings in the spring and summer and sow the seeds in spring.

Thymus vulgaris

Common Thyme

A well-known and important herb, common thyme is a perennial sub-shrub and is still used in the kitchen after many centuries to flavour meat, fish and vegetable dishes, in *bouquets garni*. It is a charming, attractive plant for the herb container and a 'lawn' composed of carpeting thymes of mixed colours and textures looks spectacular in bloom. Thymes will cascade over a low wall and if planted between paving slabs, they will spread and soften the edges.

There are a number of thymes that can be used in the kitchen including *T. herba-barona*, with the scent of caraway traditionally used to flavour a baron of beef, and some creeping thymes.

Care

Thymes thrive in extremely dry conditions, most preferring a gritty or gravelly soil in direct sunlight. Surround creeping thymes with a layer of sand, gravel or small stones placed on the soil's surface so that the mat of leaves is kept dry and clean. Lightly trim back bushy thymes after they have flowered.

New plants

The many creeping thyme varieties can be easily propagated by division. Most of the 'decorative' thymes do not produce seed or do not come true from seed.

Viola tricolor

Heartsease

Heartsease, or Johnny-jump-up, is a delightful wildflower that blooms continuously all summer and well into the autumn. It readily cross-pollinates with other violas to produce a wide range of colour combinations. Hundreds of varieties of violas and violettas are available from specialized growers and suppliers. This is a delightful small flower for the container gardener, as it can be planted around the edges of the containers to provide long-lasting colour and interest.

Heartsease self-seeds everywhere. It will thrive in the rock garden, in gravelly or sandy areas, and in a border or even a formal herb garden. It enjoys hot sun.

Medicinally it was used as a blood purifier, for fevers, as a gargle, and to treat ulcers and sores. It is fed to racing pigeons as a tonic and blood purifier. The dainty little blooms can be sprinkled on green salads.

Care

Heartsease grows best in fertile to sandy loam. It enjoys a site in full sun.

New plants

Sow seed in spring in containers in a cold frame. Take tip cuttings in summer, if wanted. The plant self-seeds freely.

DIRECTORY

Medicinal Herbs

Acanthus mollis

Acanthus

Sometimes known as bear's breeches, acanthus is a stately plant. Its tall spikes of mauve-and-white flowers make a stunning sight in summer, and the dark green, glossy, deeply divided leaves are highly decorative – in fact, they inspired ancient Greek architectural embellishment. The plant was also used medicinally by the ancient Greeks.

Acanthus is a specimen plant. Grow it so that the fine foliage and the magnificent flower spikes can be seen to best advantage. It looks wonderful in an island bed or border, where the surrounding plants should be much lower growing.

In regions where acanthus will not survive the winter, it can be grown successfully in a large container. In the first winter especially, it is necessary to give the plant a deep mulch, from 15cm (6in), of leaves, bracken, straw or similar material to protect it from freezing temperatures.

Care

Acanthus likes well-drained, loamy soil and a site in full sun, although it will tolerate partial shade.

New plants

Sow seeds in spring; divide in autumn or spring; take root cuttings in winter.

H 1.2m (4ft)
S 45cm (18in)

15–17°C
(60–62°F)

Direct sunlight

Achillea millefolium

Yarrow

Yarrow is an aromatic perennial. The attractive foliage is made up of thousands of tiny leaves (hence the name millefolium).

Since it seeds profusely, yarrow must be kept within bounds. Seed heads should be cut off before they ripen and at this stage can be hung up to dry and used in decorative dried arrangements. This plant is a good subject to naturalize in an area of wild grasses.

Yarrow was once used as a wound poultice in ancient times. Many of its common names refer to its ability to stem the flow of blood. It is also valuable as a remedy for fever and as a digestive tonic. A useful dye plant, it produces browns and greens.

Care

Yarrow prefers poor, well-drained soil. It is a good plant for chalky and seaside gardens. It prefers a site in full sun, although it will tolerate partial shade.

New plants

Sow seeds in spring; divide in spring or autumn; take softwood cuttings in early summer.

Agastache foeniculum

Anise Hyssop

This native of the north American prairies is a beautiful plant with anise-scented leaves and decorative spikes of mauve-purple flowers. It is often known as *A. anethiodora*, or blue giant hyssop.

Anise hyssop is an excellent flower for beekeepers since it attracts honey-bees and bumblebees. It also looks stunning planted in a border or island bed with other herbs and wild plants. Unfortunately, anise hyssop is short lived and it is best to take a few cuttings every year to ensure that it is not lost over the winter.

The fresh or dried leaves of the plant are used for flavouring and for tea. The dried flowers are a good ingredient for potpourri. The herb also has medicinal properties and a leaf tea is used for fevers, coughs and colds.

Care

This plant is happiest in well-drained loam situated in direct sunlight.

New plants

Sow the seeds in the spring.

Ajuga reptans

Bugle

Bugle has shiny dark green and purple, oval leaves and spikes of purple-blue flowers. It is a densely spreading plant that makes a superb ground cover. There are several extremely decorative forms, such as 'Atropurpurea' (beet-coloured leaves), 'Burgundy Glow' (magenta leaves edged with cream), and 'Variegata' (grey-green leaves edged with cream).

In the garden bugle requires a moist and humus-rich soil, and in hot regions some shade from the sun. It will grow well through gravel, provided there is good soil and some moisture underneath, and it thrives in a damp area near a pond, in a hedgerow, or in shade.

Bugle was traditionally known as the carpenter's herb, as it was used to stop bleeding.

Care

Bugle prefers humus-rich, moist to damp soil and a site in full sun, although it will tolerate partial shade.

New plants

Sow seeds in summer and autumn (germination can be erratic); plantlets produced by runners.

Alchemilla vulgaris

Lady's Mantle

Lady's mantle makes a dense ground cover. This attractive herb is often used to edge a border, especially to fall over hard paving. Trim the flower heads back after blooming; the plant will then continue to flower through the summer.

The species usually grown in gardens is *A. mollis*, from Asia Minor. It is vigorous and has hairy leaves that give it a softer look. There are also several low-growing alpine species, including *A. alpina*, which are excellent for the rock garden.

An important medicinal herb in the 16th century, lady's mantle is now used to treat menstrual and digestive disorders. The dried flower heads of all species look good in flower arrangements.

Care

Lady's mantle should be grown in a deep loam in order to thrive. It requires a site in full sun, although it will tolerate partial shade.

New plants

Sow seeds in spring to early summer. Divide roots in spring or autumn; self-seeds.

Althaea officinalis

Marsh Mallow

As its name suggests, the beautiful herb marsh mallow, also known as mallard, grows in damp places. A tall, stately plant with an abundance of grey-green, soft, velvety leaves, it bears masses of delicate pink flowers in late summer. The seed heads resemble small, flat, round 'cheeses', in which each seed forms a segment.

The marsh mallow looks attractive growing near water or in clumps at the back of an island bed or border, where its muted foliage makes a backdrop for other brighter flowers. It is an excellent feature plant, too.

Marsh mallow, in common with most other members of the mallow family, has since earliest times been used for food, and all parts of the plant are edible. The roots were once used to make the sweets known as marshmallows; they can also be cooked as a vegetable, and the young leaves and shoots may be eaten in salads.

Medicinally, this herb has been valued for its soothing properties to treat inflammation, coughs, bronchitis and hoarseness. Externally, the leaves are used as a poultice and to relieve the pain and swelling of bee stings.

Care

Marsh mallow prefers rich, moisture-retaining to damp soil. It thrives in salty seaside conditions and a site in full sun.

New plants

Sow seeds in spring (germination can be erratic); take cuttings in early summer; divide roots when dormant.

Althaea rosea

Hollyhock

The hollyhock was introduced from China in the 16th century. It comes in a diverse range of flower colours, from white and the palest shades to rich reds, pinks and a deep purple-black. There are also double forms. It is a stately plant that looks good, and grows best, against a wall. Hollyhocks love good drainage and thrive in brick and lime rubble.

In suitable conditions hollyhock self-seeds readily. It is this random seeding that produces the groups of hollyhocks with flowers of different shades that are so appealing.

Hollyhock has similar medicinal properties to *A. officinalis*. The flowers are used as a tisane to treat chest complaints, or as a mouthwash.

Care

Hollyhocks need a well-drained soil in a site in full sunlight.

New plants

Sow seeds in spring or late summer; self-seeds.

Arctostaphylos uva-ursi

Bearberry

Bearberry is also commonly known by its Latin name of uva-ursi. This evergreen herb is an attractive ground-cover plant, with small, shiny, dark green leaves and tiny, pink-tipped, white flowers followed by red berries in the autumn. Bearberry grows best where there is no chalk in the soil and prefers acid conditions. If there are conifers in the garden, it will greatly enjoy the dappled shade beneath them where the tree litter is acidic.

This herb has important medicinal properties which are particularly valued by herbal practitioners in the treatment of urinary, bladder and kidney infections, but should not be used for home treatment. The berries yield ash-grey and blue dye.

Care

Bearberry likes light, humus-rich, rather dry to sandy soil, with some moisture. It prefers a site in direct sunlight, although it will tolerate partial shade.

New plants

Sow seeds in the autumn; layer shoots, and take greenwood cuttings in summer.

Arnica montana

Arnica

Also called mountain tobacco, arnica is a much-valued perennial herb in medicine and arnica ointment is used to treat bruises and sprains. It is also used in homeopathy to treat epilepsy, high blood pressure and shock. As with all medicinal herbs, it should not be used in its natural state for the plant is poisonous and toxic and can cause skin irritation. It is not a large plant and carries attractive yellow flowers. It is a popular plant for growing in containers.

Care

Arnica prefers humus-rich, acid, sandy soil and an open, sunny site.

New plants

Sow fresh seeds in autumn or early spring; divide in spring.

Atriplex hortensis var. *rubra*

Red Orache

Red orache is an arresting herb with a deep red stem and purple-red leaves. A single plant in rich soil will grow to a substantial size with several stems and will make an impressive architectural feature plant if given space around it. It self-seeds profusely if allowed, and seedlings will appear the following spring. Orache is also available in golden-leaved and green-leaved forms, both of which are very decorative in the garden.

Orache is also known as mountain spinach, which indicates its culinary use. Young leaves may be added to salads, cooked like spinach, or made into a soup. For use as a vegetable, the plant must be given plenty of water when growing or the leaves will be tough. Medicinally orache was used to treat sore throats and jaundice. At the end of the season, dry the seed heads for winter arrangements.

Care

This plant requires moisture-retaining, fertile loam and a site in full sun.

New plants

Sow seeds in late spring or autumn.

Calendula officinalis

Pot marigold

Pot marigold is one of the most colourful of all perennial herbs and among the easiest to grow. The plant often seeds itself, but seeds can be sown in spring, and the plants will be in full flower during summer. Pot marigold really brightens up the herb garden and can be grown equally well in a flower border or an island bed. It looks much more natural grown as an individual plant rather than en masse. These plants used to be grown as a vegetable but have fallen from favour as the leaves are rather bitter. Young leaves can be used in salads and the flowers can be sprinkled on salads and soups as decoration. They can also be dried and used as a colouring or a substitute for saffron. Medicinally, pot marigold was used as an antiseptic and in the treatment of gangrene.

Care

Pot marigolds will thrive in loam and most garden soils. This plant will tolerate dry conditions and prefers a site in full sun.

New plants

Sow seeds *in situ* in spring. Thin seedlings to 15cm (6in) apart.

Chrysanthemum parthenium

Feverfew

Once known as flirtwort, this native of southeastern Europe has now spread far afield in gardens and naturalized in the wild over most of Europe and North America. Feverfew is a multi-branched plant; the masses of white daisy-like flowers have yellow centres. The whole plant is strongly aromatic, and the leaves are bitter to taste.

In the garden feverfew looks its best in a large group and thrives in well-drained or even dry locations. It spreads extensively from seed if not cut down after flowering.

Feverfew has a long tradition as a medicinal herb to treat fevers, indigestion, and is also a sedative. In recent years this herb, taken in tablet form or as fresh leaf, has assumed new importance in the treatment of migraine and arthritis and is now a registered medicine in Britain, where it has been extensively researched. The dried leaves are also useful in the home as a moth repellent.

Care

Feverfew prefers well-drained soil of any type. It requires a site in full sun, although it will tolerate partial shade.

New plants

Sow seeds in spring or late summer; self-seeds.

Cimicifuga racemosa

Black cohosh

Black cohosh, also known as black snakeroot and bugbane, was once considered to be effective in treating snakebites and also to have insect-repellent properties. It is an imposing plant, with tall wiry flower stems that move even in the slightest breeze, and attractive foliage.

This is a plant that loves a shady site, some moisture in the soil, and generally cool conditions. It will tolerate some sun. Grow cohosh under trees or in the shade of a wall, fence or hedge. It dislikes competition and should be given space to develop.

The dried rhizome of the plant is used medicinally only by herbal practitioners as an antispasmodic and pain reliever.

Care

Black cohosh prefers humus-rich, moisture-retaining loam. It requires a site in shade or partial shade.

New plants

Sow seeds in the autumn when they are fresh. Divide in spring.

Warning This plant is potentially toxic. Use under medical supervision only and avoid during pregnancy.

Digitalis

Foxglove

The stately foxglove is one of our best-loved and most elegant wildflowers. It often occurs in large, dramatic stands in woodland clearings, sometimes in profusion on roadsides, and even on rocky hillsides.

This herb can be grown in a wide range of situations in the garden and is very adaptable, but it looks best in a fairly shady position, against a dark background created by trees or shrubs. Foxgloves always look stunning, whether planted in large stands or growing singly as graceful specimens. They produce tens of thousands of dust-like red-brown seeds and self-seed readily. If they are cut down after flowering to avoid seeding, they will sometimes live for another year.

The properties of foxglove leaves as a heart tonic were discovered in 1785, and it has played an important role in medicine ever since. Foxglove is, however, poisonous and should not be used except by qualified practitioners.

Care

Foxgloves like well-drained, moisture-retaining loam to light sandy soil. They require a site in partial shade or shade.

New plants

Sow seeds in late summer. This plant self-seeds.

Warning This plant is poisonous.

Echinacea purpurea

Purple Coneflower

This important perennial medicinal herb is native to North America, where the dried, powdered root was used by the Plains Indians as an antibiotic to cure rabies, snakebite and septicaemia. Today it is used in homeopathic medicine and is thought to have beneficial effects, boosting the immune system. With their petals radiating from a prominent centre, coneflowers are rather like giant daisies, to which family they belong. The name comes from the Greek word echinops ('hedgehog'), an allusion to the bristles on the bracts of the flowers.

Care

Purple coneflower prefers fertile, well-drained soil that retains some moisture in summer. It requires a site in full sun, although it will tolerate partial shade.

New plants

Sow seeds in late spring or early summer at 21°C (70°F); divide in spring or autumn.

Eupatorium purpureum

Joe-pye weed

Joe-pye weed is a charming name for this spectacular, tall North American plant, sometimes called queen of the meadow. However, Joe-pye weed is not a meadowland plant; instead it grows in open woods, scrub and at the water's edge, on moist soils, although it tolerates drier situations.

Joe-pye weed is more impressive than its close relative, the European hemp agrimony. It looks its best at the rear of a border with shrubs and trees as a backdrop. Alternatively, it can be planted with dramatic effect in moist ground by a pond or stream. It is very attractive to bees and butterflies.

Traditionally this herb, along with the spotted Joe pye, was used by the Indians and later by the first settlers to treat fevers. Today it is used in the treatment of urinary stones, gout and rheumatism by qualified herbalists.

Care

Joe-pye weed prefers a rich, moist, calcareous loam and a site in full sun, although it will tolerate partial shade.

New plants

Divide in spring or autumn; sow seeds in spring.

Galium odoratum

Sweet woodruff

This herb is a woodland plant and should always be grown in the shade, as in bright sunlight the wonderful effect of the tiny, pure white flowers that are set against the decorative green foliage is lost. It is the perfect ground-cover plant, growing well among trees and shrubs, where it forms a dense, bright green carpet over the soil, suppressing most weeds. In good soil that is treated with leaf mould and has sufficient moisture, woodruff will romp away.

Woodruff seed is covered in tiny hooked bristles which catch onto animal coats for wider distribution. The seed is difficult to germinate: it should be sown fresh in the autumn and requires cold and frost to break its domancy. It germinates in spring.

Sweet woodruff has been used since ancient times, particularly as a strewing herb. When dried it smells wonderfully of new-mown hay, and it also has insect-repellent properties. As a medicinal herb, woodruff is a source of coumarin for anticoagulant drugs. A tea made from the plant relieves stomach ache but is also a delicious drink.

Care

Plant sweet woodruff in humus-rich, moisture-retaining soil in shade.

New plants

Sow fresh seeds in late summer and divide after flowering.

Galium verum

Lady's Bedstraw

The herb lady's bedstraw is also known as yellow bedstraw and cheese rennet, since it was once used for stuffing mattresses and also has the property of curdling milk.

This herb will thrive in poor dry soil and is particularly at home near the sea. In certain areas of North America it has become a weed. Lady's bedstraw should be grown in a mass for the full dramatic effect of its tiny golden flowers and incredible honey scent. It is a good plant for clothing a dry bank or growing in poor ground, and can be mixed with suitable meadow grasses and other flowers of dry grassland to make a natural meadow.

A decoction of the dried flowers was used medicinally for urinary conditions and was once considered a treatment for epilepsy. The roots yield a lovely red dye similar to that produced by its relative, madder.

Care

This plant will do well in most well-drained soils. It requires a site in full sun, although it will tolerate partial shade.

New plants

Sow seeds or divide plants in autumn or spring.

Gentiana lutea

Yellow Gentian

The spectacular yellow gentian produces many spires of brilliant yellow flowers with a hint of orange. It is not the easiest plant to grow and from seed will take at least three years to flower. When plants are raised, they should be transplanted young, since the yellow gentian puts down a long taproot, often several feet in length.

Plant the herb in the shady border in a small group. Provide it with a deep, alkaline soil that is well drained but still retains moisture. The taproot helps the plant survive drought.

The long thick root of yellow gentian is used to make tonic bitters for treating loss of appetite, and as a general tonic for the digestion. When seed has set, the dried stems of the plant make striking decorations.

Care

Yellow gentian prefers deep, well-drained but moisture-retaining loam. It requires a site in partial shade.

New plants

Sow seeds in autumn; divide mature crowns in spring.

Hamamelis virginiana

Witch Hazel

Other names for this small tree are spotted alder, winterbloom and snapping hazelnut. The form of its growth is shrub-like, with several twisting stems coming from the base. It flowers in the depths of autumn and winter, after the leaves have fallen. Although each spider-like flower is quite small, a mature witch hazel in full bloom is highly decorative. The foliage turns a rich golden yellow in the autumn. Japanese and Chinese species are showier, with larger flowers.

Witch hazel will grow in partial shade, but in the garden it looks better in an open position, in full sun at the back of a border.

North American Indians used a decoction of witch hazel medicinally. Today its astringent properties are valued both medicinally and as additions to cosmetic preparations.

Care

Witch hazel like moist, humus-rich soil, which is preferably neutral to acid. It requires a site in full sun, although it will tolerate partial shade.

New plants

Sow seeds in autumn; take softwood cuttings in summer.

Humulus lupulus

Hop

If you see a hop plant twining through a country hedge, you will notice that it is a very vigorous plant. Hop is easily grown from seed but it is best to buy female plants. Their flowers are decorative and have the medicinal and flavouring properties, but they produce seed only if grown with the male plant. The large dark leaves will quickly cover an old shed or climb a tall tree, and there will be a great display of cones to harvest.

Today the hop is employed as a safe and effective sedative – hence the use of hop pillows. The dried flower heads make attractive winter decorations. The strong, flexible vine is used in Scandinavia as a fibre to make cloth, and in basket making.

Care

Hops prefer humus-rich and moist or moisture-retaining soil which is well drained. It requires a site in full sun, although it will tolerate partial shade.

New plants

Sow seeds in autumn; take cuttings in early summer.

Hypericum perforatum

St John's Wort

St John's wort is an attractive plant that can be grown in a border or against a wall, but looks its best among other wild plants in a natural area. In certain climates it can become a weed. St John's wort yields a profusion of tiny brown, resin-scented seeds which, in ideal conditions, produce thousands of seedlings.

This herb is the only member of the genus used medicinally, in both herbal and homeopathic medicine. The plant has vulnerary, sedative, antiviral, antidepressant, antibiotic and diuretic properties. Its leaves are used to treat wounds, bruises, burns and painful joints. The flowers yield a dye which turns silk and wool a violet-red but will not dye cotton.

Care

St John's Wort grows well in most well-drained soils. It likes a site in full sun, although it will tolerate partial shade.

New plants

Sow seeds in autumn or spring; divide plants in the autumn.

Inula helenium

Elecampane

Elecampane is a stately, impressive plant grown for its ample foliage as well as its sunflower-like blooms. This herb will provide structure and architectural focus to a planting so give it plenty of space. In winter it disappears completely.

The plant seeds profusely. Cut the heads before the seeds are ripe or it could become a nuisance. The seed heads are beautifully marked once the seed has been cleaned out, and make good dried winter decorations.

Elecampane has been used as a medicinal herb since ancient times. The plant is a bactericide and tonic. The dried root is valued in the treatment of respiratory disorders. Elecampane is still used in the manufacture of some wines and liqueurs. The flowers yield a yellow dye and the roots give a blue.

Care

Elecampane is suited to any fertile, moisture-retaining soil. It requires a site in full sun to partial shade.

New plants

Sow seeds in spring or when ripe; divide rootstocks in the autumn.

Lobelia syphilitica

Great Lobelia

Great lobelia is often used as a medicinal substitute for *L. inflata* (Indian tobacco), an annual of no great decorative value. Great lobelia, on the other hand, is a handsome and colourful plant and is useful in the garden because it flowers so late – at the summer's end, when flowering plants are becoming scarce. It can be grown in any good soil that retains moisture, but in its natural habitat it is associated with water. Grow it in the bog garden or near the edge of a pond, where its roots will search out moisture throughout the summer. In a large clump it will give welcome colour when other waterside flowers have stopped blooming.

As its Latin name indicates, this was a herb that the Iroquois Indians employed to treat venereal disease: they made the root into a tea. Leaf tea was also employed for colds, fevers and stomach trouble.

Care

Great lobelia grows best in rich, moist or moisture-retaining soil. It requires a site in full sun.

New plants

Sow seeds in spring, surface sow.

Lythrum salicaria

Purple Loosestrife

Purple, or spiked, loosestrife is a handsome waterside plant for the pond, though in warm climates it can be invasive. In parts of North America it has taken over, and should always be introduced with caution.

The long purple flower stems look stunning beside water and produce thousands of tiny red-brown dust-like seeds. This plant should always be encouraged to form a good stand.

Purple loosestrife is still valued in herbal medicine; it has tonic, antibacterial and hemostatic properties. The plant rapidly stops bleeding, is a good wound cleanser, and makes an effective gargle.

Care

Purple loosestrife prefers a fertile, moist or wet soil. It should be planted in a site in full sun, although it will tolerate partial shade.

New plants

Sow seeds or divide in spring.

Marrubium vulgare

Horehound

Useful in the herb garden for its distinctive texture and colour, horehound's soft silvery-green foliage and 'frosted' appearance have a subtle charm. It is an undemanding plant to grow and prefers the poorest conditions. Take advantage of its drought-resistant qualities.

Horehound is a useful foliage plant that blends well with a wide range of herbs and makes an attractive foil for brighter-coloured flowers.

In England horehound beer was formerly very popular and sweets were made from the juice of the plant. Medicinally the herb's greatest value is in the treatment of bronchitis, coughs and sore throats and as a bitter digestive tonic.

Care

Horehounds need well-drained, sandy, dry and poor soil in order to thrive, in a site in full sunlight.

New plants

Take cuttings in summer; divide roots in spring; stratify seed and sow in spring or autumn. Germination can be erratic.

Mentha x piperita

Peppermint

Peppermint is used in flavouring and also in cosmetics and soaps. It is quite a large perennial and reaches 90cm (36in) in height. It can be planted in containers where its red stems and crisp, red-tinted leaves look attractive. It is the most valuable of all the mints medicinally. Fields of peppermint are grown commercially, and the essential oils distilled for a number of uses. In England the centre of the peppermint industry used to be the town of Mitcham in Surrey. The plant is a hybrid of *M. aquatica*, watermint, and *M. arvensis*, cornmint.

Mints have hairy leaves which can cause skin irritations and rashes. Handle them with care. Similarly, mint tea should not be drunk continuously over a long period.

Warning All mints spread vigorously and do best in fertile, well-drained soil that retains moisture. They need to be contained and the traditional way of doing this in the garden was to plant them in an old bucket sunk into the soil with the bottom removed.

Care

Peppermint needs well-drained, moisture-retentive soil and an open, sunny site.

New plants

Divide runners in autumn. Never attempt to grow any mint from seed as the varieties are unlikely to breed true.

Monarda

Bergamot

Wild bergamot enjoys being in dryish soils but is a woodland-edge plant, so give it some shade from the hottest midday sun and grow it in a situation where trees, shrubs, or a hedge form a background feature. For a striking effect plant wild bergamot in a good size clump. Grow it with other drought-tolerant herbs that enjoy light shade such as *Galium verum* (lady's bedstraw), *Origanum vulgare* (wild marjoram) and the popular *Digitalis grandiflora* (yellow foxglove).

Monardas can easily be propagated by 6–10cm (3–4in) tip cuttings taken from late spring to late summer. The roots of mature plants can also be divided into smaller sections to make new plants. Try to divide them every two or three years.

Care

Monardas like to be planted in well-drained, dryish loam or sandy soil in partial shade, although they will tolerate full sun for most of the time.

New plants

Sow seeds in the spring. Take cuttings from late spring to late summer and divide plants in the autumn or spring.

Oenothera biennis

Evening Primrose

Evening primrose is something of a misnomer as, although many species open their flowers at dusk, they are often open for much of the day, especially in cloudy weather. Their wonderful, intense fragrance is most noticeable at night. The tall *O. biennis* is most suited to any dry situation or stony ground, where a selection of evening primroses can be grown.

Evening primrose has recently become an important medicinal herb used to treat premenstrual syndrome, multiple sclerosis and other conditions. The thick root of the plant has been used as a vegetable.

Care

Evening primrose prefers well-drained soil and a site in full sunlight.

New plants

Sow seeds in late summer; self-seeds.

Ruta graveolens

Rue

Rue, once called the herb of grace, has long been used medicinally. It is a decorative garden plant, particularly the variety 'Jackman's Blue', which has more ample, blue-green foliage and blends particularly well with silver and grey herbs.

It will grow on the poorest, driest of soils, and although it will do well in rich, fertile soil, it will be less hardy. It enjoys a hot sunny site in the bed or border and also thrives in gravel.

Rue has long been regarded as an excellent antiflea herb. In homeopathic medicine it is used as an ointment for sprains and strains. It is too powerful to use as a home remedy.

Care

Rue needs well-drained, calcareous and not too fertile soil and a site in full sunlight.

New plants

Sow seeds in spring; take cuttings in early summer.

Warning Rue can cause a phototoxic rash. Wear gloves when handling, especially in sunlight.

Scutellaria lateriflora

Skullcap

Skullcaps grow all over the world although the majority are native to North America. The plant is known as mad-dog skullcap in the USA, where it was considered a treatment for rabies. The name skullcap comes from the miniature seed capsule, which opens like a helmet when the seed is ripe and ready for dispersal.

The mad-dog skullcap is a modest plant whose main use in the garden is a ground cover in moist, shady areas among trees and shrubs. It spreads rapidly in damp soils by pale yellow underground runners. There are many other species, some of which are well worth growing in the garden.

The plant is now considered an effective medicinal for the treatment of the nervous system, on which it acts as a tonic.

Care

Skullcap prefers moist to moisture-retaining, fertile loam. It requires a site in shade, although it will tolerate partial shade.

New plants

Sow seeds or divide plants in spring.

Symphytum x uplandicum

Russian Comfrey

Grow Russian comfrey in a plot of its own for use in composting. Well-manured, it can be cut down up to six times a season. Other species also make attractive garden plants: *S. grandiflorum*, with creamy-pink flowers, produces excellent ground cover; *S. peregrinum* has intense blue flowers; and *S. orientale* bears cream-coloured blooms.

Comfrey, also known as knitbone, boneset and bruisewort, is an old and valuable medicinal plant. A leaf poultice is used externally for bruises, burns, wounds and ulcers, and a leaf tea given for gastric ulcers, pleurisy and bronchitis.

Care

Russian comfrey likes rich, moisture-retaining loam. It needs a site in full sunlight, although it will tolerate partial shade.

New plants

Sow seeds in summer or autumn; divide roots in spring.

Warning This plant is phototoxic.

Valeriana officinalis

Valerian

Valerian, also known as all-heal, is an old medicinal plant whose use dates back to the 10th century.

It is very ornamental, with masses of frothy pink flowers and attractive foliage, and looks its best planted near water, alongside other herbs from a similar habitat. Valerian will spread and form a large clump in time. It self-seeds to a limited extent.

Medicinally valerian is used as a herbal tranquilizer to treat insomnia, hypertension, nervous exhaustion and anxiety. Herbal preparations that contain valerian are widely favoured in Europe. In the USA, however, this natural medicine is prohibited.

Care

Valerian prefers fertile, moist to moisture-retaining loam. It should be situated in direct sunlight, although it will tolerate partial shade.

New plants

Sow seeds in spring; divide roots in spring or autumn.

Verbena officinalis

Vervain

Considered a sacred herb by the Romans, vervain was used to purify homes and temples and was traditionally employed as a cure for dropsy. In England it is commonly found growing by roadsides and in sunny pastures.

The aerial parts of the plant are used as an effective nerve tonic, liver stimulant, urinary cleanser and fever remedy. They are also traditionally used to encourage milk flow and can be taken during labour to encourage contractions.

Vervain also has a number of topical uses, including on sores, wounds and gum disorders. It is also used to encourage sweating and to stimulate the immune system in feverish conditions.

Care

Vervain prefers fertile, moist to moisture-retaining loam. It should be situated in direct sunlight, although it will tolerate partial shade.

New plants

Sow seeds in spring; divide roots in spring or autumn.

DIRECTORY

Ornamental Herbs

Dipsacus fullonum

Teasel

The teasel is a tall, and imposing plant with distinctive spiny flower heads which bloom in a unique way. The flowers form a band around the head, spreading up it, at no time covering it completely. The flowers are attractive to insects, particularly bees. The light green leaves form a deep cup which fills with dew and rainwater.

Teasel should be seeded on waste ground by a stream or on a bare bank or other empty area. It will seed itself profusely if allowed.

Fuller's teasel (*D. fullonum* subsp. *fullonum*) is famous for its use in the cloth industry. The heads of this plant have bristly, hooked spines – unlike those of the common teasel – and once matured and dried, these were used to tease, or raise, the nap on woollen cloth. It is a cultivated sub-species which is well worth growing for interest. Collect all teasel seed heads when they are golden, before they are rained upon, to preserve their beautiful colour for winter decorations.

Care

Teasel likes moisture-retaining loam or clay and a site in full sunlight, although it will tolerate partial shade.

New plants

Sow seeds in late summer. This plant self-seeds.

Nepeta mussinii

Catmint

There are many catmints suitable for the herb garden. They make lovely soft edging plants, with masses of summer blooms. Catmint will flower again in the autumn if cut back after the first long flowering.

This plant looks best when it is tumbling over the edge of a path or low wall, and is suitable for planting in an open border or a rock garden. The soft grey-green foliage is a wonderful foil for brighter flowers.

N. cataria (catnip) is the traditional herbal catmint. It grows tall and bears white flowers dotted with purple and strongly scented, nettlelike leaves. Cats love this herb.

Catmint was traditionally a medicinal plant and is also used for tea.

Care

Catmint performs best in sandy or well-drained loam which is moist to dry. It requires a site in full sunlight, although it will tolerate partial shade.

New plants

Sow seeds or divide plants in spring; take cuttings in early summer.

Polemonium caeruleum

Jacob's ladder

Jacob's ladder is so called because of the ladder-like formation of its bright green leaves. This is a cottage flower that has been grown for many centuries in country gardens.

Jacob's ladder requires moisture in the soil to flourish and grows well in full sunlight or partially shaded areas. It associates well with water, and with trees and shrubs. For a long flowering, cut down the stems before they go to seed. One stem will be more than adequate for self-seeding, since seeds are produced in abundance.

In times past the herb was used to treat fevers, headaches, epilepsy and nervous complaints.

Care

Jacob's ladder prefers humus-rich, moist to moisture-retaining, calcareous loam. It requires a site in full sunlight, although it will tolerate partial shade.

New plants

Sow seeds in spring or autumn; divide roots in spring; self-seeds.

Glossary

Annual A plant that completes its cycle of germination from setting seed through dying in a single growing season.
Aromatic Having a strong, volatile, fragrant odour.
Astringent Dries, tightens or shrinks tissue, stops discharges.

Biennial A plant requiring two growing seasons to flower and seed.
Bulb A plant storage organ, usually formed underground, containing the following year's growth buds.

Coagulant Helps the blood to clot.
Corm A swollen stem base that acts as a storage organ, similar to a bulb.
Cultivar A man-made or cultivated variety, produced by hybridization.
Cutting A section of a plant removed for propagation.

Division The splitting of a plant clump into various sections containing roots and shoots; normally done when the plant is dormant, for purposes of propagating or reinvigorating the plant.

Emollient Softens and soothes, usually externally.
Expectorant Loosens and discharges phlegm.

Flower head A mass of small flowers that appear as one flower.
Force (-ing) A method of promoting early flowering or fruiting, usually via artificial heat and light.

Half-hardy A plant that withstands low temperatures but not freezing.
Hardy A plant that tolerates year-round conditions in temperate climates, including normal frost, without protection.
Herbaceous A non-woody plant that dies down to its rootstock in winter.

Hybrid A plant resulting from crossing two different species.

Laxative Stimulates and quickens the involuntary muscular contractions of the digestive tract, or moistens the colon, to relieve constipation.
Layering A method of pinning a stem to the ground and inducing it to form roots, thereby propagating a separate plant.

Mulch A layer of organic or inorganic material added to the surface of the soil to retain moisture, help suppress weeds and gradually improve fertility.

Node The point at which a leaf grows from the stem.

Offset A plant that is reproduced naturally from the base of the parent plant.

Perennial A plant that lives for longer than two seasons.
Prostrate Growing flat along the ground.
Purgative Strongly cathartic, produces vigorous emptying of the colon.

Rhizome An underground, often creeping, stem acting as a storage organ, from which roots and shoots grow.
Rootball The roots together with the soil adhering to them when a plant is lifted, e.g. for transplanting.

Sedative Calms or relaxes the nervous system – reduces nervousness, distress, or irritation.

Type Used to refer to an original plant species.

Variety A variant of a plant species, arising either naturally or as a result of selection.
Vulnerary Helps heal wounds and sores, usually applied externally.

Index